Git for Programmers

Master Git for effective implementation of version
control for your programming projects

Jesse Liberty

BIRMINGHAM - MUMBAI

Git for Programmers

Producer: Ravit Jain
Acquisition Editor – Peer Reviews: Saby Dsilva
Content Development Editor: Alex Patterson
Technical Editor: Gaurav Gavas
Project Editor: Namrata Katare
Copy Editor: Safis Editing
Proofreader: Safis Editing
Indexer: Pratik Shirodkar
Presentation Designer: Ganesh Bhadwalkar

First published: June 2021

Production reference: 1240621

Published by Packt Publishing Ltd.
Livery Place
35 Livery Street
Birmingham B3 2PB, UK.

ISBN 978-1-80107-573-2

www.packt.com

Foreword

Git is powerful, but complex. Many developers, myself included, use it daily but get pretty worried when we get outside of our comfort zones. After that, it's off to copy and paste internet search results and hope for the best… Or we might just clone to another folder and merge our changes by hand. Tell me I'm not the only one who does that from time to time, hoping it goes well so we don't have to quit our job and leave the country under the cover of night.

Part of the problem is that Git has a ridiculous number of rarely used commands, each with a long list of options. There are websites that will generate fake Git command documentation (search for "git man page generator" for an example), and it's hard to tell them apart from the real thing. Type the wrong Git command and you might lose your code changes, get stuck in vim (requiring a reboot to exit), upset your co-workers by pushing to the wrong branch, publish your passwords to GitHub, or even end up with a detached head (a truly terrifying prospect).

And, let's be honest, another part of the problem is that no one wants to look stupid. Everyone is expected to be a Git expert now, but most developers will admit (under conditions of strict anonymity) that they're not. So it can be a little embarrassing to ask for help.

You're in luck – this book is here to help!

I've had the honor of knowing Jesse for at least a decade. Maybe longer – both of our memories get fuzzy past the decade range. We've been co-workers, co-presenters, co-podcasters, co-authors, and also great friends. We both turn to each other for advice. Like many in the community, I've come to trust Jesse to break down complicated concepts to the essentials, and explain them in a way that just makes sense – and, quite often, surprise us by making the whole process a lot of fun.

Jesse has outdone himself with this book. It's well designed and expertly written. When he told me that he was writing a book on Git, I honestly thought, "Good luck with that…" because there's just so much to cover, but he's done an amazing job of figuring out the truly important concepts, focusing on them, and just nailing the explanations.

He's kept things "as simple as possible, but no simpler" as the quote (often attributed to Einstein) goes. There are some places where you need to know some Git internals to understand what you're doing, and Jesse explains those well, but he doesn't waste your attention with trivia.

A few of my favorite sections of the book:

The chapters on rebasing, amending, cherry-picking, and interactive rebasing really helped me more deeply understand what those commands are doing. I had some "cargo cult" commands that mostly seemed to work for me, but I couldn't have explained what they were actually doing. Jesse's diagrams and examples made a lot of lightbulbs go on for me there.

Some of the final chapters covering aliases, log, stash, and bisect gave me a lot of tips to work more effectively.

The *Fixing Mistakes* chapter is an amazing list of hands-on steps to get yourself out of common Git emergencies, and Jesse explains what the commands are doing. I absolutely see myself diving for this chapter the next time Git threatens to detach my head.

And finally, the challenges at the end of each chapter are an amazing resource. After learning the content in a chapter, these challenges (with detailed answers to follow) give you some fun puzzles to test your knowledge. I plan to revisit the challenges periodically to test my retention and read up on the solutions to fill in the spots I've forgotten.

Congratulations to you on picking a great book to take your Git knowledge to the next level, and to Jesse for proving me wrong and writing an amazing book about Git.

Jon Galloway

Senior Program Manager on the .NET Community Team

Contributors

About the author

Jesse Liberty is a Principal Software Engineer at StoryBoardThat. He is the author of two dozen programming books and a not-yet-published novel, as well as over two dozen training videos for Pluralsight, Packt, and Udemy.

Jesse is an international speaker and blogger (jesseliberty.com) and he is the host of the popular Yet Another Podcast, which you can access through his web site: jesseliberty.com/podcast.

He has been programming for 30 years (starting in 8086 Assembly and C!) and in C# since 2001. He is currently focused on .NET 5/6, C# 9, and related technology (Git, Azure DevOps, etc.).

When he is not programming… just kidding. He's always programming.

There are too many people to thank, but let's begin with the folks at Packt. Others, in no particular order, include: Namrata Katare, the people at StoryBoardThat, Mads Torgersen, Scott Guthrie, Scott Hanselman, Bill Wagner, Jared Parsons, Brent Laster, Jon Galloway, John Papa, Ward Bell, Adam Summers, Seth Weiss, Stacey Liberty, Skip Gilbrech, Dan Hurwitz, the folks in the Microsoft MVP program, the Albahari brothers, Douglas Crockford, Julie Lerman, Andrew Lock, Ken Henderson, and all the others I've forgotten.

About the reviewers

Wilson Mar has been trying to figure out Git and GitHub since 2010. In 2020 he helped to migrate 3,000 developers and their repositories to GitHub.com. He collects PROTIPs at his blog, https://wilsonmar.github.io.

Johannes Schindelin has been involved in the Git project since 2005. He invented the interactive rebase and is the maintainer of Git for Windows.

Table of Contents

Preface

This is a book about Git, the most popular version control system in the world. I will explain what version control is and then lead you from introductory topics to quite advanced material. See chapter 1 for what background experience and software you will need (all free).

Who this book is for

This book is for programmers of any skill level. Full Stop.

Version control is essential to every programming project, as will be explained in chapter 1, and Git is the world's most popular version control system. The larger the team the more urgent it is that you use version control, but it can be essential for a single programmer as well.

What this book covers

Chapter 1 is the *Introduction*; you will learn about how the book is structured, what Git is, what version control systems are, where Git came from, and what tools are available for Git. You will also learn how to install Git on your computer.

In *Chapter 2*, *Creating Your Repository*, you will learn how to create a repository and clone it from GitHub. You will see the relationship between the repository on your disk and the one you've created on GitHub. A simple example program will be introduced.

In *Chapter 3*, *Branching, Places, and GUIs*, we'll cover the work area, the index, the repository, the remote repository, and the stash; what they are; and what they are for.

In *Chapter 4, Merging, Pull Requests, and Handling Merge Conflicts*, you'll learn about branching: a central concept in version control and one of Git's great strengths. Branching allows you to work on more than one thing at a time and keeps your release code clean. Git has especially fast branching.

In *Chapter 5, Rebasing, Amend, and Cherry-Picking*, you'll learn how to re-write history with Rebase and Amend. The very term Rebase makes some programmers quiver with fear, but I'll show you how to master this useful (and safe!) tool.

In *Chapter 6, Interactive Rebasing*, we'll look at how you can change the message associated with your commit, rearrange multiple commits, and even drop commits before pushing them to the server.

In *Chapter 7, Workflow, Notes, and Tags*, we examine the basic workflow for managing your repository, as well as how to add metadata to keep your repository clean and clear.

In *Chapter 8, Aliases*, we'll examine aliases and how they can save you a lot of work. Aliases can combine commands and all their flags to make your life much easier.

In *Chapter 9, Using the Log*, we will look at the very powerful `log` command. Log is much overlooked, and yet it can give you insight into every aspect of your current and past status of your projects.

In *Chapter 10, Important Git Commands and Metadata*, we'll go on to examine some very useful and important Git commands. These powerful statements can get you out of trouble when things appear to have gone wrong.

In *Chapter 11, Finding a Broken Commit: Bisect and Blame*, we'll look at a life-saving command, `Bisect`, which helps Git help you find where your program broke.

In *Chapter 12, Fixing Mistakes*, you'll learn how to get yourself out of difficulty if you make a mistake while using Git.

Finally, in *Chapter 13, Next Steps,* we'll take a quick look at additional resources.

To get the most out of this book

- You will want to be somewhat comfortable with a programming language. Familiarity with C# is a big plus, but not required.

- You will need Git (free) installed on your computer, and it would be best also to have the latest free version (or better) of Visual Studio 2019. Finally, you'll want to download and install (free) GitHub Desktop. Thus, you do not have to spend any money to follow the examples in this book.

- A note to macOS users: All of the above applies to you as well, and I don't anticipate you having any additional issues.

- A note to Linux users: I don't work with Unix, but I strongly suspect that all of the above (except Visual Studio) will apply to you as well.

Download the color images

We also provide a PDF file that has color images of the screenshots/diagrams used in this book. You can download it here: `https://static.packt-cdn.com/downloads/9781801075732_ColorImages.pdf`.

Conventions used

There are a number of text conventions used throughout this book.

`CodeInText`: Indicates code words in text, database table names, folder names, filenames, file extensions, pathnames, dummy URLs, user input, and Twitter handles. For example: "If you look at the log, `git log --oneline`, you should see all three commits: the one created when you cloned the repository and the two you created by hand."

A block of code is set as follows:

```
public int Add (int left, int right)
{
    return left + right;
}
public int Subtract (int left, int right)
{
    return left - right;
}
```

When we wish to draw your attention to a particular part of a code block, the relevant lines or items are set in bold:

```
public int Add (int left, int right)
{
    return left + right;
}
public int Subtract (int left, int right)
{
    return left - right;
}
```

Any command-line input or output is written as follows:

```
git add .
git commit -m "Add calculator class"
```

Bold: Indicates a new term, an important word, or words that you see on the screen. Words in menus or dialog boxes appear in **the text like this**. For example: "Select **System info** from the **Administration** panel."

 Warnings or important notes appear like this.

Get in touch

Feedback from our readers is always welcome.

General feedback: If you have questions about any aspect of this book, mention the book title in the subject of your message and email Packt at customercare@packtpub.com.

Errata: Although we have taken every care to ensure the accuracy of our content, mistakes do happen. If you have found a mistake in this book, we would be grateful if you could report this to us. Please visit www.packtpub.com/support/errata, select your book, click on the **Errata Submission Form** link, and enter the details.

Piracy: If you come across any illegal copies of our works in any form on the Internet, we would be grateful if you would provide us with the location address or website name. Please contact us at copyright@packtpub.com with a link to the material.

If you are interested in becoming an author: If there is a topic that you have expertise in and you are interested in either writing or contributing to a book, please visit http://authors.packtpub.com.

Share your thoughts

Once you've read *Git for Programmers*, we'd love to hear your thoughts! Scan the QR code below to go straight to the Amazon review page for this book and share your feedback.

https://packt.link/r/1-801-07573-5

Your review is important to us and the tech community and will help us make sure we're delivering excellent quality content.

1

Introduction

In this chapter, we will cover the following topics:

- A very brief history of version control and Git
- Getting and setting up Visual Studio 2019, GitHub Desktop, and your terminal
- Getting and installing Git
- Configuring Git for Visual Studio, GitHub Desktop, and GitHub at the command line

Let's get started!

About this book

> *"Begin at the beginning," the King said gravely, "and go on till you come to the end, then stop." – Alice in Wonderland*

In this book, we will cover Git from the very beginning all the way through to advanced topics. No experience with Git is expected. Though if you have been using Git, you'll probably want to skim the initial chapters. Git is arguably the most popular version control system in the world, but this raises the question: "What is version control?"

Version control

Before version control, I would code a bit and then when I became afraid of losing that code, I would make a backup of my directory. This is slow, inefficient, takes up a lot of disk space, and is very hard to share with others.

A **Version Control System** (**VCS**) does all this work for you (and more) and does so in a way that is fast, efficient, and takes up a minimum of disk space. One of the fastest and most efficient is Git, although there are others. This book will not spend a lot of time convincing you that Git is better than the others. First, the market has spoken, and Git prevails. Second, if you've purchased this book, you've already decided. And if you haven't already purchased this book, go do so. I'll wait here.

About the code examples

In order to demonstrate the use of Git, we need to have a small program that we can evolve. The code examples are given in C#, but they are so simple that you'll be able to follow them regardless of your experience with the language. For example, if you can figure out what this does, you're all set.

```
public class Program
{
    public void PrintHello()
    {
        Console.WriteLine("Hello World!");
    }
}
```

This code declares a class (don't worry about what that is) named Program. Inside that class is a method (function) called PrintHello that prints Hello World to the console (your screen).

This is about as complex as it gets, and I'll explain each code snippet as we go.

Just a brief history

In July of 2005, after just a few month's work, Linus Torvalds, the genius behind Linux, released Git to meet his own needs, the needs of the Linux community, and eventually, the rest of us. The goal of Git was to be fast and efficient. It succeeded.

While most VCSes at the time were centralized (all the files were kept on a big server), Git uses a distributed system, in which everyone has their own repository. Technically, no central server is required for Git, although if you are working in a team, a central place for sharing code is convenient. But the huge difference is that with Git, the vast majority of your interactions with the VCS are local – right there on your disk.

Tools for working with Git

There are a number of easily confused terms (such as Git versus GitHub) and there are many tools for working with Git – from the command line to **Graphical User Interface (GUI)** tools. This section will review some of these options.

GitHub, et al.

There are many services that allow you to create shared "repositories" (the location of all the versions of your program). The most famous and popular are GitHub and Microsoft's Azure, as well as BitBucket and GitLab. Azure is a very powerful system for DevOps, while GitHub is a very straightforward way to host your program. We'll be using GitHub in this book. (Recently, Microsoft acquired GitHub for $7.5 billion in stock – and made a huge commitment to GitHub, open source and, of course, to Git.)

 Key point: Git is the system we're covering in this book. GitHub is a central repository system for sharing code (we'll make this more specific later in the book) and GitHub Desktop is a GUI for working with Git.

GUIs and the command line

There are many ways in which to interact with Git. The principal ones are to work at the command line or to use a GUI. There are a wide number of GUIs. This book will focus on GitHub for Desktop and Visual Studio 2019, as well as the command line. In fact, one of the things that makes this book different is that all of Git will be explained using these three tools. This will give you a deep understanding of Git along with how the GUIs can help (and can hinder) your work.

There are many other excellent GUI tools, and the ecosystem of tools keeps evolving. That said, the ones we will use are both powerful and representative of what you get with nearly all the other GUI tools. In addition, these tools are well established and likely to stick around. Furthermore, if you learn one GUI and see how it relates to command-line instructions, you'll find it easy to use other GUIs.

We will look first at the command-line interface to Git. While there are some limitations in GUI tools, if it can be done with Git, it can be done at the command line, that is, all of Git's functionality is exposed at the command line. Furthermore, as has often been pointed out, understanding Git at the command line will make your use of a GUI much easier as you will know what is actually happening.

Does it help to understand how your car works? Not at all, until something goes wrong. Then you turn to the expert mechanic who can fix the problem. In Git, the expert is the programmer who knows the command line.

The command line

Out of the box, on Windows 10, the command line is available straight from your terminal. It gives you everything you need, but it is a bit ugly:

```
C:\GitHub\gitProgrammers>git status
On branch main
Your branch is up to date with 'origin/main'.

Changes to be committed:
  (use "git restore --staged <file>..." to unstage)
        new file:   gitProgrammers/gitProgrammers.sln
        new file:   gitProgrammers/gitProgrammers/Program.cs
        new file:   gitProgrammers/gitProgrammers/gitProgrammers.csproj


C:\GitHub\gitProgrammers>
```

Figure 1.1: Git at the command line

It is hard to read, but we can make it pretty, so that it's easier on the eye.

Making the command line pretty

If you are using Git on Windows 10, you can make the command line prettier and more useful, as shown here:

```
C:\GitHub\gitProgrammers          ×    +   ∨
SESA560987@DESKTOP-D21661F ▶ C:\GitHub\gitProgrammers    main ≡ +3 ~0 -0 ~
> git status
On branch main
Your branch is up to date with 'origin/main'.

Changes to be committed:
  (use "git restore --staged <file>..." to unstage)
        new file:   gitProgrammers/gitProgrammers.sln
        new file:   gitProgrammers/gitProgrammers/Program.cs
        new file:   gitProgrammers/gitProgrammers/gitProgrammers.csproj

SESA560987@DESKTOP-D21661F ▶ C:\GitHub\gitProgrammers    main ≡ +3 ~0 -0 ~
> _
```

Figure 1.2: Example of Pretty Print

To do this, download and install Power Shell. Then, follow Scott Hanselman's excellent directions at `http://jliberty.me/PrettyGit`.

A similar effect can be had on mac and Linux by following the directions at `https://github.com/diogocavilha/fancy-git`. There are other options available on the GitHub site that do pretty much the same thing.

Visual Studio 2019

Visual Studio 2019 has extensive support for Git built in. There is a separate menu specifically designed for Git, and Git information is integrated into the general UI:

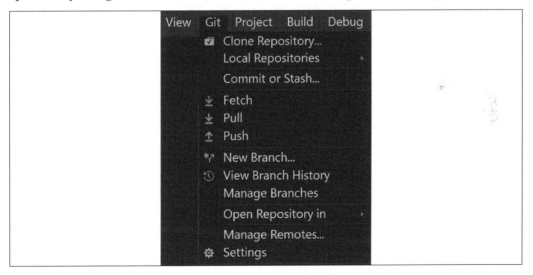

Figure 1.3: Git menu in Visual Studio 2019

The first order of business is to get and set up Visual Studio.

Getting Visual Studio for free

All three of the products used for illustration purposes in this book (the command line, Visual Studio 2019, and GitHub Desktop) have free versions available. To obtain your copy of Visual Studio 2019, go to http://visualstudio.com and hover over the **Visual Studio** button. Select **Community 2019**. It will download and all you have to do is double-click on it and follow the instructions:

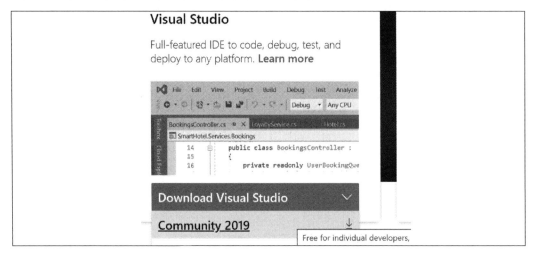

Figure 1.4: Obtaining Visual Studio

If you are using a Mac, there are some significant differences between how Visual Studio 2019 for Windows handles Git and how Visual Studio for Mac does. You will probably have no trouble following along, but you can always use the Terminal or GitHub Desktop.

GitHub Desktop

A very popular GUI, especially for use with GitHub, is GitHub Desktop. This cross-platform application makes working with Git extremely easy: anticipating what you might want to do and making that simple. The downside is that there are limitations, as there are for virtually every GUI.

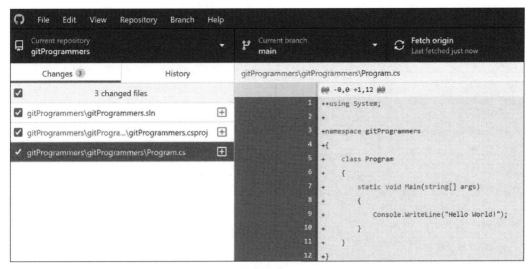

Figure 1.5: GitHub Desktop

We will be using all three of these throughout the book: command line, Visual Studio 2019, and GitHub Desktop. As we proceed, the selections and Git commands shown above will make much more sense; for now, just get a feel for their appearance.

Getting Git

The very first thing you need to do is to install Git on your computer. The official Git site states that "even if Git is already installed on your computer, it is probably a good idea to reinstall to update to the latest version."

Getting Git on Windows

There are also a few ways in which to install Git on Windows. I recommend using the official build. The most recent one is available from the Git website: https://git-scm.com/download/win.

Another way to get Git, and to kill two birds with one stone, is to download and install GitHub Desktop. The installer will also install a command-line version of Git. You can get it at https://desktop.github.com/:

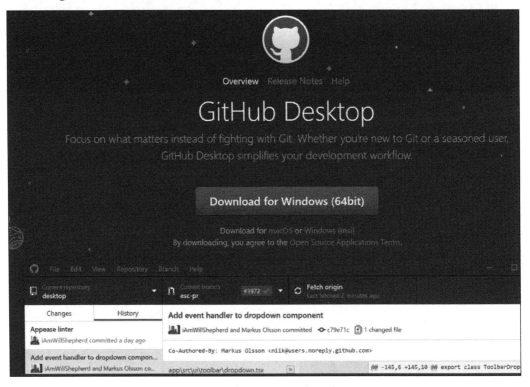

Figure 1.6: Obtaining GitHub Desktop

This book will show its demonstrations on Windows 10, using Git version 2.30.0.windows.2, but the examples should work with just about any version of Git.

Getting Git on a Mac

There are several ways to install Git on a Mac. The easiest is probably to install the Xcode command-line tools. You can do this by trying to run Git from the Terminal the very first time, as follows:

```
$ Git --version
```

If you don't have it installed already, it will prompt you to install it.

If you want a more up-to-date version, you can also install it via a binary installer. A macOS Git installer is maintained and available for download at the Git website at `https://git-scm.com/download/mac`:

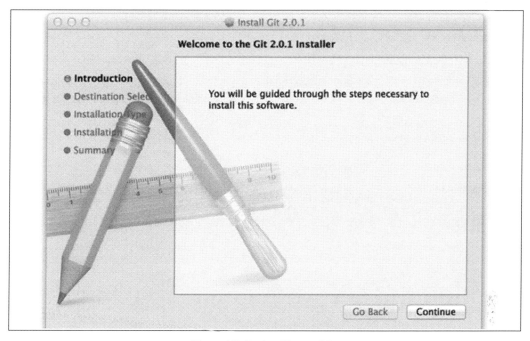

Figure 1.7: Getting Git on a Mac

You can also install it as part of the GitHub Desktop for macOS install. Their GUI Git tool also has an option to install command-line tools. You can download that tool from the GitHub Desktop for macOS website at `https://desktop.github.com`.

Getting Git on Linux

This book does not formally support Linux, but almost all of Git is the same on all platforms.

If you want to install the basic Git tools on Linux, you can generally do so through the package management tool that comes with your distribution. If you're on Fedora (or any closely related RPM-based distribution, such as RHEL or CentOS), you can use `dnf`:

```
$ sudo dnf install git-all
```

If you're on a Debian-based distribution, such as Ubuntu, try apt:

```
$ sudo apt install git-all
```

Checking your version

Once you have Git installed, your first command should be the following:

```
git --version
```

That is, the keyword git, and then version, preceded by two dashes. This is sometimes called "git dash dash version."

The output on my computer is as follows:

```
> Git --version
git version 2.30.0.windows.2
```

(Your mileage may vary.)

Configuring Git – the command line

We'll look at configuring Git to personalize throughout this book, but for now, let's add your name and email address so that every entry into Git is stamped appropriately. Enter the command-line command:

```
git config --global --edit
```

This will bring up your editor. Find or create the [user] section and add the following:

```
[user]
name = Jesse Liberty
email = jesseliberty@gmail.com
```

You will probably want to use your own name and email address.

There are other entries in the config file. Ignore them for now and save and close the file.

Configuring Git – Visual Studio

In Visual Studio for Windows, click on the Git menu and a dialog box will open. On the first tab, enter your username and email address:

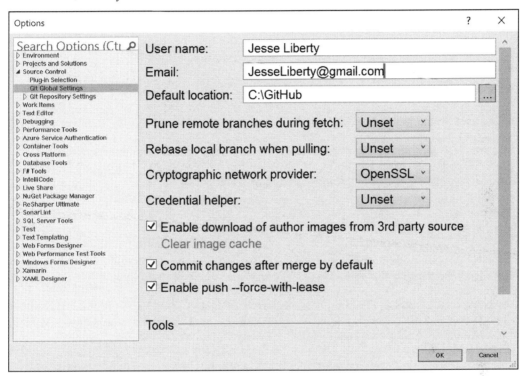

Figure 1.8: Setting Git options in Visual Studio

Configuring Git – GitHub Desktop

To configure GitHub Desktop, you'll need an account on GitHub. We'll cover that in the next chapter. Once you do have an account, go to **File | Options**, select the **Accounts** tab, and then click on **Sign in**:

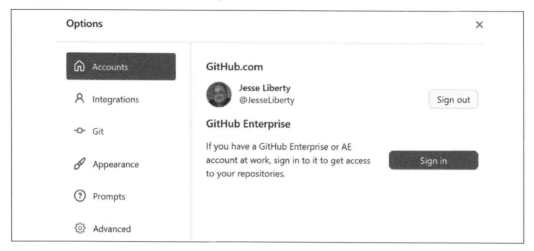

Figure 1.9: Setting up GitHub Desktop

Summary

In this chapter you saw an introduction to the book, listing what is in each chapter. You also saw a quick history of version control and of Git itself.

Next, we took a look at downloading the environments you'll need to follow along: Visual Studio 2019, GitHub Desktop, and PowerShell as your command line. All of these can be obtained for free.

Once the software was downloaded, we looked at how to set up Git, and how to set up the tools we'll be using.

2
Creating Your Repository

In this chapter, you will learn how to create an account on GitHub, and how to create and clone your first repository so that you have a link between the repository on your computer and that on GitHub.

This chapter will cover:

- Creating your repository
- Git pull
- Push me, pull you
- Starting at the command line
- Commits – best practices

We'll start by creating your GitHub repository.

Creating your repository

There are a number of different ways to create your repository. We'll cover creating a repository on GitHub and cloning it to your disk, as this is the most common way.

Creating your repository on GitHub first

Your first step is to register with GitHub. Go to http://github.com and click **Sign Up**. Fill in your username (it will tell you if the name is taken) and your email and it may ask you to verify that you are a human. Assuming you are, click **Create Account**.

Fill out their micro-survey and click **Create Account**. You will be asked to verify your email, and once you do, you'll see the (one-time) opening page asking what you want to do first. Choose **Create a repository**:

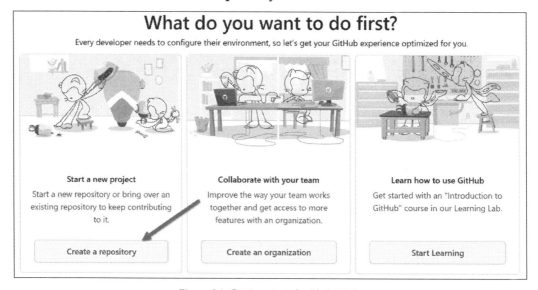

Figure 2.1: Getting started with GitHub

If you already have an account, sign in and press **New Repository**. You may not find this at first glance, in which case click the big plus sign in the corner.

Either way, you will be brought to the **Create A New Repository** page. The first job is to give your new repository a name. I'll use ProGitForProgrammers. Feel free to use any name you want as long as GitHub doesn't complain that the name is taken.

Now it is time to fill in the form:

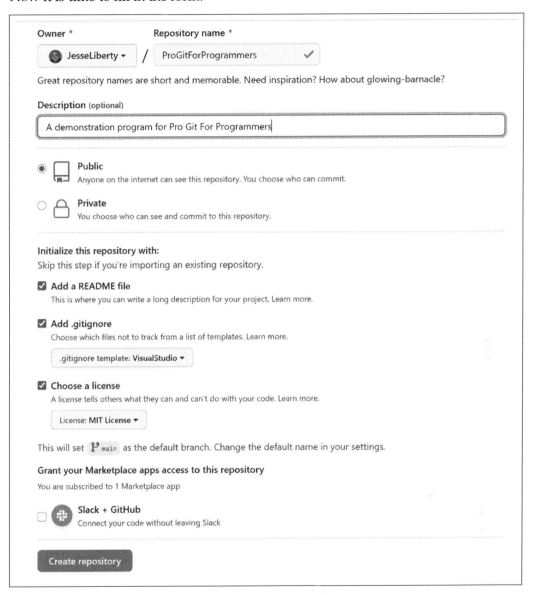

Figure 2.2: Creating the repository

Start by entering a short description of your project. Next, and very importantly, choose whether you want this repository to be public (anyone can see it) or private (only people you invite can see it).

I strongly recommend checking **Add a README file**. This will be what is shown to users when they come to your repository. You can fix the file up later using Markdown.

Be sure to add a .gitignore file. This tells Git which files to ignore when checking your files into the repository. This can be very important so that you don't overwrite another programmer's metadata files. Click the dropdown and admire how many languages are supported; for C# I recommend you search for and choose Visual Studio.

If your repository is public, be certain to choose a license for the code. I chose the MIT License. You can learn more about this license at https://opensource.org/licenses/MIT.

That's it! You are ready to click **Create repository**. When you do, you'll be brought to the home page for your new GitHub repository:

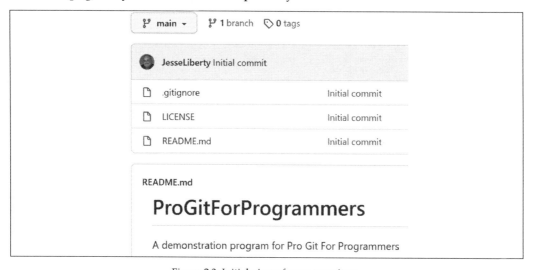

Figure 2.3: Initial view of your repository

Notice that you have the three files you asked for, and that you can see a preview of the README as well as the description you entered.

Right now, this repository exists only on the server. You want to put a copy on your disk so that you can add code and use commands to keep them in sync. Therefore you will "clone" the repository; that is, you'll make an exact copy of the remote repository in your local repository.

How you will do this will depend on whether you are using the command line, Visual Studio, or a GUI.

Cloning to your computer – command line

Cloning to your local repository is easy. Open your terminal (or PowerShell) and change the directory to where you want the repository to go (in my case GitHub/the command line).

Switch back to your GitHub repo on GitHub.com, and see the green button in the upper right-hand corner marked **Code**. Click that button and a small dialog box will open. Choose **HTTPS** unless you know you have **SSH** (as I do). In either case, click on the clipboard icon to copy the address:

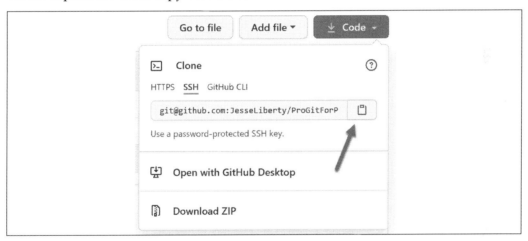

Figure 2.4: Copying the address of the repo

Return to the command line, enter git clone, and then paste in the address:

```
git clone git@github.com:JesseLiberty/ProGitForProgrammers.git
```

You should see something like this:

```
SESA560987@DESKTOP-D21661F ▶ C:\GitHub\CommandLine
❯ git clone git@github.com:JesseLiberty/ProGitForProgrammers.git
Cloning into 'ProGitForProgrammers'...
remote: Enumerating objects: 5, done.
remote: Counting objects: 100% (5/5), done.
remote: Compressing objects: 100% (5/5), done.
remote: Total 5 (delta 0), reused 0 (delta 0), pack-reused 0
Receiving objects: 100% (5/5), done.
SESA560987@DESKTOP-D21661F ▶ C:\GitHub\CommandLine
❯ _
```

Figure 2.5: Cloning at the command line

Change the directory to ProGitForProgrammers and you'll see that the three files that were on the server are now here as well:

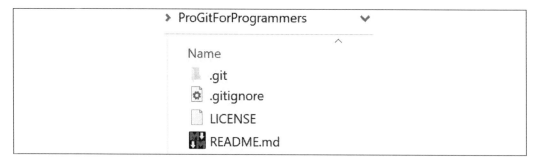

Figure 2.6: Files in the directory

Now let's take a look at how to do this in Visual Studio.

Cloning to your computer – visual studio

Go to your directory (in my case GitHub) and make a directory called VisualStudio.

Open Visual Studio with no project. Select **File | Clone Repository**. Fill in the fields and click **Clone**:

Figure 2.7: Cloning to your local repository using Visual Studio

A few seconds later you will see the three files, now shown in the **Solution Explorer**:

Figure 2.8: Cloned files in Visual Studio

There are a number of ways to clone from a GitHub repository to your own. One way is to use a dedicated GUI tool such as GitHub Desktop.

Cloning to your computer – GitHub for Desktop

Once again, return to your root directory (GitHub) and make a new directory. This time call it GitHubDesktop.

Now, return to GitHub and click **Code**:

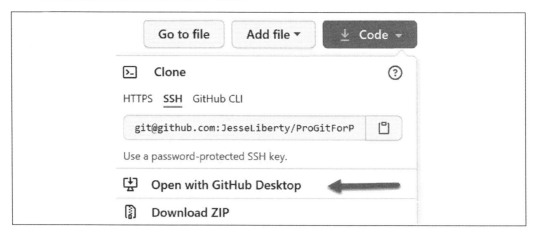

Figure 2.9: Cloning directly through GitHub Desktop

Notice that one of the choices is **Open with GitHub Desktop**. Click on that. A dialog will open. The only field you need to fill in is the local path. Click **Clone**:

Figure 2.10: Cloning to GitHub Desktop using HTTP

Notice that GitHub Desktop wants the `https` URL for your repository.

You now have three copies of your original repository, each in its own directory: `CommandLine`, `VisualStudio`, and `GitHubDesktop`. These might represent three programmers working on the same solution, or various ways for one programmer to choose to clone their project.

Creating a project

We need a project. Using Visual Studio (or your favorite editor) create a project called `ProGitForProgrammers` in the `CommandLine` directory. When you are done, you should have the three original files and a folder for your program. In that folder will be the `.sln` file as well as a folder for the code.

Open the command line and navigate to the same directory. When you get there your command line should look something like this:

Figure 2.11: The command-line prompt

Look at the yellow, where you see +1 ~0 -0. The +1 means you've added a file or a directory; the ~0 indicates that no files have been modified; the -0 indicates that no files have been deleted. Let's see what was added. Enter:

```
git status
```

You should see something like this:

```
> git status
On branch main
Your branch is up to date with 'origin/main'.

Untracked files:
  (use "git add <file> ..." to include in what will be committed)
        ProGitForProgrammers/

nothing added to commit but untracked files present (use "git add" to track)
SESA560987@DESKTOP-D21661F  ▶ C:\GitHub\CommandLine\ProGitForProgrammers  ⑂ main ≡ +1 ~0 -0 !
>
```

Figure 2.12: Untracked files

Git is telling you that you are on the branch `main` (the only branch for now) and that you have "untracked files" – that is, files that are in the directory but that are not being tracked by Git. If they are untracked, Git can't store them; in fact, Git knows nothing about them. Let's fix that. Enter these commands:

```
git add ProGitForProgrammers/
git commit -m "First commit - from command line"
```

add tells Git that this is a file it should pay attention to and `commit` brings it into the local repository.

Every `commit` must have a message, and if you don't provide one, you'll be prompted by Git to add one. Here I've added it by using the -m flag.

Once again, all this is happening locally and so GitHub doesn't know about it. We can fix that by pushing our commit up to the server:

```
git push
```

Now if you go to GitHub and refresh the page your project will be there. You can click your way down through the folders, and even into `Program.cs`, to see the code:

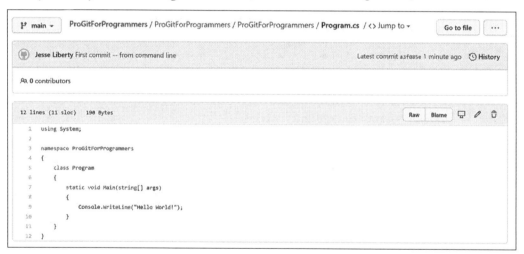

Figure 2.13: Viewing your code on GitHub

Notice in the upper left that it tells you that you are on the **main** branch. Next to that is the path to get to `Program.cs`. Below that is the message you added, and then the file itself.

Git pull

Having pushed your commits to the server, other developers may want to pull them to their own directory, to keep in sync.

Pulling down using GitHub Desktop

Having put the project up on the server, we can simply pull it down into the other locations. For example, open GitHub Desktop. It will tell you that there have been changes in the repository and helpfully offer a button for you to update your local repo.

If you open a file explorer and navigate to the GitHubDesktop directory, you'll see that there is now a replica of the files you pushed from the command line.

Pulling down to Visual Studio

Click on the Git menu and choose **Pull**. Visual Studio is updated with the code from the server. Now all three repositories are up to date. This is the heart of Git:

- Save your files to a local repository
- Push your files to the remote repository
- Pull down any files that are on the remote repository but not on your local repository

Push me, pull you

Generally, you want to push your changes and pull down changes from other developers. Also, generally, you will not be working on the same files, and certainly not in main. We'll discuss how to avoid this in *Chapter 4, Merging Branches*. For now, we'll just be very careful.

Open Visual Studio in the directory GitHub/VisualStudio/ProGitForProgrammers. Add a line to Program.cs as shown here:

```
namespace ProGitForProgrammers
{
    class Program
    {
        static void Main(string[] args)
        {
```

```
        Console.WriteLine("Hello World!");
        Console.WriteLine("I just added this in Visual Studio");
    }
  }
}
```

Having made your change, you want to check it in. Since we are in the `VisualStudio` directory, we'll do the work right within Visual Studio. Click the `Git` menu and choose **Commit or Stash**. A Git window will open as a tab next to **Solution Explorer**. Enter a commit message and press **Commit All**:

Figure 2.14: Git window in Visual Studio

 Note that if you drop down the **Commit All** menu, you have a number of shortcuts for adding, committing, and pushing your changes.

As you can see, and will see often in this book, you can do almost anything in Visual Studio that you can do at the command line.

Pushing to the server

You have now committed your changes to your local repository. The GitHub repository, however, doesn't know about your changes. (You can prove this to yourself by returning to GitHub and drilling down to `Program.cs`.)

The other programmers' repositories (for example, `CommandLine` and `GitHubDesktop`) are equally oblivious. To disseminate this change, you first push your changes up to the server (GitHub) and then pull them down to the other repositories.

From within Visual Studio's Git window, press **Staged**. This will stage your changes for committing. Next, click **Commit**. This will put your changes into your local repository (be sure to give the commit a meaningful message).

Examine the Git window; there is a lot of information:

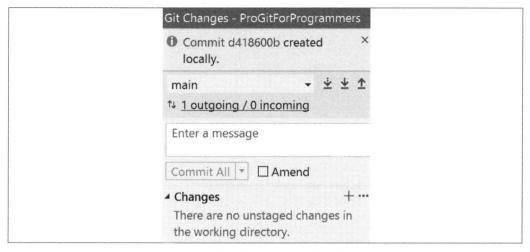

Figure 2.15: The Git window in Visual Studio

You are told that the commit was created locally (and locally is the important part!). Below that is the status of your commit. You have one to push up to the server (outgoing) and none to bring down (incoming):

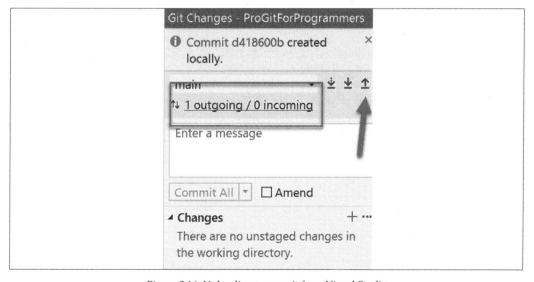

Figure 2.16: Uploading a commit from Visual Studio

Now, find the up-pointing arrow in the upper-right corner. Hover over it and you'll see that it says Push. Click that button to push your changes to the server. When it is done, it will give you a success message. Ignore the offer to create a pull request for now.

Look to the left of your Git menu and see the local history of your commits:

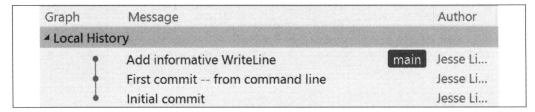

Figure 2.17: The history of commits

Each dot signals a commit, and next to each dot is your commit message (and now you can see why meaningful commit messages are both hard to write and worth the effort). There is also an indicator that main is pointing to your last commit.

If you check GitHub (remember to refresh the page) you will now see the line in Program.cs. Make sure you understand why: this is because after we committed the change, we pushed it to the remote repository.

Downloading the changes at the command line

We created the changes in the VisualStudio directory. CommandLine and GitHubDesktop know nothing of the changes, even though they are now on GitHub.

For these directories to know about the changes, you need to pull the changes down.

Change directories to CommandLine. Examine the contents of Program.cs; the new line is not there. Open your terminal and enter pull. This will pull any changes from the server to your local repository.

The result should look like this:

```
> git pull
remote: Enumerating objects: 8, done.
remote: Counting objects: 100% (8/8), done.
remote: Compressing objects: 100% (2/2), done.
remote: Total 5 (delta 3), reused 5 (delta 3), pack-reused 0
Unpacking objects: 100% (5/5), 474 bytes | 12.00 KiB/s, done.
From github.com:JesseLiberty/ProGitForProgrammers
   a3f085e..d418600  main         -> origin/main
Updating a3f085e..d418600
Fast-forward
 ProGitForProgrammers/ProGitForProgrammers/Program.cs | 1 +
 1 file changed, 1 insertion(+)
SESA560987@DESKTOP-D21661F ▶ C:\GitHub\CommandLine\ProGitForProgrammers   ⑂ main ≣
```

Figure 2.18: Pulling from the remote repository

Git is telling you that it formatted and compressed your files and passed them down to your repository. Toward the bottom it says that it used Fast-forward. We'll discuss this in *Chapter 4, Merging, Pull Requests, and Handling Merge Conflicts.*

Take a look at Program.cs now in your command directory; the new addition should now be there.

 Want to do something cool? Open the Program.cs file before updating. After the update you will see the second WriteLine pop into view. What is actually happening is that the code that was in your directory is replaced by the new code on the pull.

Downloading the changes using GitHub Desktop

Change directories to GitHubDesktop and open the GitHub Desktop program. It will give you a lot of information about the status of your repository (**No Local Changes**) and it will automatically check and inform you that there is one commit to update your local repository with:

Figure 2.19: The view from the remote repository

Go ahead and click **Pull origin**. It does the pull, and the button disappears. Check your code; the change should now be in your Program.cs (and is recorded in your local repository).

 All three local repositories and the server repository are now in sync.

Starting at the command line

You can start the process at any of our repositories. Last time we started in the VisualStudio repository and then pulled the changes down to the CommandLine and GitDesktop repos. This time, let's start at the command line.

Open Visual Studio and point it to the project in your CommandLine directory. Just to be certain, right-click on **Solution**, select **Open Folder in File Explorer**, and make sure you are in the right directory.

To keep this example very simple, we'll just add another line to Program.cs:

```
class Program
{
    static void Main(string[] args)
    {
        Console.WriteLine("Hello World!");
        Console.WriteLine("I just added this in Visual Studio");
        Console.WriteLine("I just added this in the command line repo");
    }
}
```

Normally you would make many more changes before checking in, but again, this is a demo and we're more interested in using Git than we are in fussing with this silly program. Save all your files and at the command line get the status by entering:

```
git status
```

This will give you output that looks like this:

```
SESA560987@DESKTOP-D21661F ▶ C:\GitHub\CommandLine\ProGitForProgrammers ⟩ ⸝ main ≡ +0 ~1 -0 !
⟩ git status
On branch main
Your branch is up to date with 'origin/main'.

Changes not staged for commit:
  (use "git add <file>..." to update what will be committed)
  (use "git restore <file>..." to discard changes in working directory)

no changes added to commit (use "git add" and/or "git commit -a")
SESA560987@DESKTOP-D21661F ▶ C:\GitHub\CommandLine\ProGitForProgrammers ⟩ ⸝ main ≡ +0 ~1 -0 !
⟩ _
```

Figure 2.20: The command line indicating one file has been modified

The key piece of information is the modified file. That is just as it should be, as that is the file we modified. You can now add it to the index and then commit it:

```
git add ProGitForProgrammers/ProGitForProgrammers/Program.cs
git commit -m "Add writeline indicating we are in command line"
```

On the other hand, you can combine these two steps with the -a flag:

```
git commit -a -m "Add writeline indicating we are in command line"
```

You will want to draw a distinction between untracked files and modified files. Untracked files are outside of Git and cannot be manipulated inside Git until they are added; modified files are tracked by Git but have changed since the last commit.

If we are happy with the commit we've added, we can (optionally) push it to the server:

```
SESA560987@DESKTOP-D21661F ▶ C:\GitHub\CommandLine\ProGitForProgrammers ⸝ main ↑1
⟩ git push
Enumerating objects: 8, done.
Counting objects: 100% (8/8), done.
Delta compression using up to 16 threads
Compressing objects: 100% (5/5), done.
Writing objects: 100% (5/5), 498 bytes | 498.00 KiB/s, done.
Total 5 (delta 3), reused 0 (delta 0), pack-reused 0
remote: Resolving deltas: 100% (3/3), completed with 3 local objects.
To github.com:JesseLiberty/ProGitForProgrammers.git
   d418600..ef16f81  main -> main
SESA560987@DESKTOP-D21661F ▶ C:\GitHub\CommandLine\ProGitForProgrammers ⟩ ⸝ main ≡
⟩ _
```

Figure 2.21: Pushing our commit to the remote repository

We'll want to do that because we want to share this code with the other programmers.

Pulling to GitHub Desktop

Switching to GitHub Desktop, we see that it already knows there is something to pull, as we saw last time. (If it doesn't, push the **Fetch** button, which will go to the server to see if there is anything to bring back.)

That's two repos that are identical, but the VisualStudio repo is not yet up to date. Let's return to Visual Studio in the VisualStudio folder.

Pulling to Visual Studio

Open the Git menu item, and select Pull. Watch your source code and see the third line pop into existence. Once again, the three local repositories and the remote repo are all in sync.

Commits – best practices

Like everything else in programming, best practices in commits are, to some degree, controversial. The first issue is frequency.

How often should I commit?

There are those who say a commit should be atomic: representing exactly one unit of work (one task, one bug fix). No more and no less. So, according to this line of thought, if you are in the middle of work and you get called away, you should not commit, but you should use the stash. The stash is an area where you can put files that you want to come back to later. You can name sets of files that you stash, and then pick the one you want to restore by name.

This is a defensible position, but I hold the opposite: commit early and commit often.

Commits are cheap and fast in Git, and interactive rebase (see *Chapter 6, Interactive Rebasing*) allows you to "squash" commits together. Therefore, if you are working on a feature and you make five interim commits before you are done, you'll have the opportunity to squash them into a single commit with a single message. This is the best of both worlds: you secure your interim work with a commit, and you present only one commit (rather than five) to the server.

Keep your commit history clean

The first way that a programmer reviews your code is to look at the list of commits and then dive into those that are interesting. A good history of commits with well-written messages is a delight to review. A long, tedious history with meaningless messages is only slightly more fun than eating glass.

A note on commit messages

As you will see later in this book, commit messages are very important for anyone (including you) reviewing your commit history. By convention, commit messages should be in the imperative, and should tell you exactly what is in that commit.

```
Fixing some files                      // bad
Fix WriteLine in helloworld.cs         // good
```

In practice you'll often find comments in the past tense:

```
Fixed WriteLine in helloworld.cs       // good enough
```

> *"In theory, theory and practice are the same; in practice, they never are."*
> *-- Pat Johnson*

It pays to get into the habit of writing good messages in the right format. Your teammates will thank you.

When the title isn't enough

The message title should be kept to 50 characters. Most of the time this is enough, but if it isn't, leave the -m message off and let Git open your editor. There you can add additional information. Skip a line after the header and consider using bullet points or other ways of making the things you want to convey easy to read.

Important: By default Git uses vi (a Unix editor). You'll want to enter:

```
git config --global core editor "code -w"
```

This ensures that Visual Studio Code is your default editor:

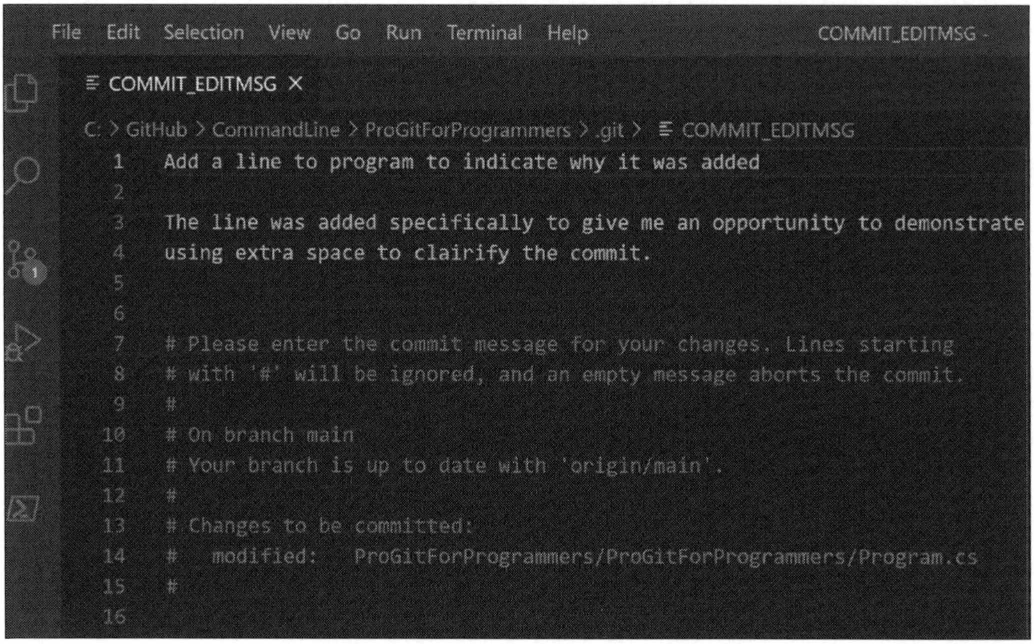

```
File   Edit   Selection   View   Go   Run   Terminal   Help                              COMMIT_EDITMSG -

≡ COMMIT_EDITMSG  ✕

C: > GitHub > CommandLine > ProGitForProgrammers > .git >  ≡ COMMIT_EDITMSG
   1    Add a line to program to indicate why it was added
   2
   3    The line was added specifically to give me an opportunity to demonstrate
   4    using extra space to clairify the commit.
   5
   6
   7    # Please enter the commit message for your changes. Lines starting
   8    # with '#' will be ignored, and an empty message aborts the commit.
   9    #
  10    # On branch main
  11    # Your branch is up to date with 'origin/main'.
  12    #
  13    # Changes to be committed:
  14    #    modified:    ProGitForProgrammers/ProGitForProgrammers/Program.cs
  15    #
  16
```

Figure 2.22: Editing in Visual Studio Code

Note that # is the comment character, and all lines that begin with # will be ignored.

When you use log (see *Chapter 9, Using the Log*) to see your history (or view history in Visual Studio, etc.) you'll see the entire message:

```
commit 4ac9d40d6f98460de31e0344cc30e660b43a459c (HEAD -> main)
Author: Jesse Liberty <JesseLiberty@non.se.com>
Date:   Wed Feb 3 14:38:12 2021 -0500

    Add a line to program to indicate why it was added

    The line was added specifically to give me an opportunity to demonstrate
    using extra space to clairify the commit.
```

Figure 2.23: The output of the log command

You can see just the headers if you want, using `git log --oneline`, but we'll leave the details for *Chapter 9, Using the Log*:

```
> git log --oneline
4ac9d40 (HEAD -> main) Add a line to program to indicate why it was added
ef16f81 (origin/main, origin/HEAD) Add writeline indicating we are in command line
d418600 Add informative WriteLine
a3f085e First commit -- from command line
a5798e1 Initial commit
```

Figure 2.24: log using the oneline flag

Summary

In this chapter, we have covered a number of topics relating to creating and interacting with your repository. We discussed:

- Creating your repository
- The relationship between your local and remote repositories
- Git pull
- Git push
- Starting at the command line
- Using Visual Studio
- Commits: best practices

In the next chapter, we'll take a look at the various places Git keeps your files, and the relationship between adding an untracked file and committing a tracked file.

3
Branching, Places, and GUIs

In this chapter, you will learn about the crucial "five places" for Git: the work area, the index, the local repository, the remote repository, and the stash. You will see how to use each of these and how they work together.

Each concept will be illustrated with both code and screenshots, and most Git actions will be illustrated in the command line, Visual Studio, and a GUI (GitHub Desktop).

You'll also learn about creating branches, committing code, and how to move commits from the work area to the repository, and from the repository to the remote repository.

Five places

As a programmer I think of Git as divided into five places:

1. The work area
2. The index (staging area)
3. The local repository
4. The remote repository
5. The stash

Let's begin by examining each of these in turn.

The work area

The work area is where your current files are. That is, if you were to open Windows Explorer and navigate to the directory you cloned to, you would see the version of the program you were currently working on. If you were to open Visual Studio 2019, these are the files that would be in the Solution Explorer. Again, the work area is where your current files are; if you open Visual Studio on your project, the files in the work area are what you will see. As you change branches (see below) the work area is updated with the appropriate files. This can be one of the hardest concepts in Git: when you change branches you change the files that are in your work area – that is, the files for that branch are swapped into the Windows (or Mac or Linux) directory.

 Note: it is possible to have more than one work area using what are known as work trees. These are well beyond the scope of this book, and you can go a long while before you will need them.

In our current program the work area looks like this in Windows Explorer:

Name	Date modified	Type	Size
bin	2/1/2021 5:16 PM	File folder	
obj	2/1/2021 5:16 PM	File folder	
ProGitForProgrammers.csproj	2/1/2021 5:16 PM	C# Project Source File	1 KB
Program.cs	2/3/2021 2:37 PM	C# Source File	1 KB

Figure 3.1: Current work area

This same directory can be seen from the command line:

```
    Directory: C:\GitHub\CommandLine\ProGitForProgrammers

Mode                 LastWriteTime         Length Name
----                 -------------         ------ ----
d----          2/1/2021   5:16 PM                 ProGitForProgrammers
-a---          2/1/2021   1:27 PM           6352 .gitignore
-a---          2/1/2021   1:27 PM           1091 LICENSE
-a---          2/1/2021   1:27 PM             77 README.md

SESA560987@DESKTOP-D21661F  C:\GitHub\CommandLine\ProGitForProgrammers   main ≡
```

Figure 3.2: Current work area from command line

In Visual Studio, the same work area looks like this:

Figure 3.3: Current work area from Visual Studio

If you look at what is in the directory, you will find the exact same files.

The index/staging area

If you have files in the work area that you would like to commit, you first add them to the staging area (often called the index). From the staging area, it takes just one command (`commit`) to move these files into the local repository.

```
class Program
{
    static void Main(string[] args)
    {
        Console.WriteLine("Hello World!");
        Console.WriteLine("I just added this in Visual Studio");
        Console.WriteLine("I just added this in the command line repo");
        Console.WriteLine("This line added to show the staging area");
    }
}
```

Figure 3.4: Modifying Program.cs

I have added a couple of lines to all three copies we have.

Let's start at the command line. I make a habit of invoking `git status` before doing anything else:

```
> git status
On branch main
Your branch is up to date with 'origin/main'.

Changes not staged for commit:
  (use "git add <file>..." to update what will be committed)
  (use "git restore <file>..." to discard changes in working directory)
        modified:   ProGitForProgrammers/ProGitForProgrammers/Program.cs

no changes added to commit (use "git add" and/or "git commit -a")
SESA560987@DESKTOP-D21661F ▶ C:\GitHub\CommandLine\ProGitForProgrammers  ⑂ main ≡ +0 ~1 -0 !
```

Figure 3.5: git status from the command line

To add this to the index at the command line, you just use the keyword `add` followed either by the name of the file or by a period (`.`) indicating you want all the files moved to the staging area:

```
git add  ProGitForProgrammers/ProGitForProgrammers/Program.cs
```

Git will make no response, but the file is now in the staging area. You can see this if you get the status again:

```
> git status
On branch main
Your branch is up to date with 'origin/main'.

Changes to be committed:
  (use "git restore --staged <file>..." to unstage)
        modified:   ProGitForProgrammers/ProGitForProgrammers/Program.cs
```

Figure 3.6: Modified file staged

This time, it shows the modified file as ready to be committed. To commit this file all you need to do is enter `git commit`. Because the file is already staged, it will be immediately committed to the local repository. If you don't add `-m "my message"` the editor will be opened for you to add your message.

Skipping the staging area

You can bypass the staging area and go directly to committing the file by using the `-a` flag. Thus, with your file unstaged you can write:

```
git commit ProGitForProgrammers/ProGitForProgrammers/Program.cs -a -m
"My message"
```

This will immediately commit `Program.cs` with the indicated message. I confess this is the way I commit files 90% of the time. (You can also use `git commit -a -m "my message"` to commit all the modified files in the working area.)

Visual Studio

In Visual Studio the status is visible at all times, in the lower right-hand corner:

Figure 3.7: Lower right of Visual Studio

The 0 with an up arrow indicates that you have no files waiting to be pushed. The 1 next to the pencil indicates that you have one modified file. Next comes the name of your program and then finally the branch you are on.

There are a number of ways to commit in Visual Studio. For example, you can commit right from the Git menu or by right-clicking on the file and selecting **Git**. You will then select **Commit or Stash**. An easier way, however, is to click on the pencil, which brings up the **Git Changes** menu:

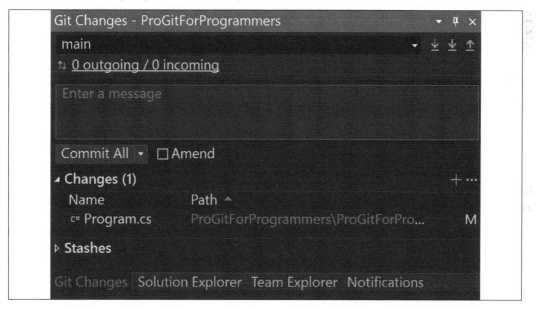

Figure 3.8: Visual Studio changes window

Here you can see the changed files and their paths. You can choose **Commit All** or drop down that button and choose from a number of related options. Fill in the message and press **Commit All** and Visual Studio immediately responds with a confirmation, reinforcement that you've committed to the *local* repository, and offers you the opportunity to upload to the remote repository (showing you that you have one outgoing file):

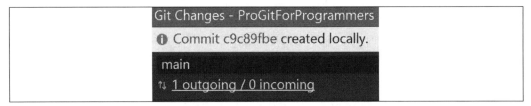

Figure 3.9: Visual Studio commit and push/pull menu

It can be confusing as to which way is outgoing as we tend to think of uploading rather than outgoing. Suffice to say that when Visual Studio says outgoing they mean going from the local to the remote server, and when they say incoming they mean moving from the server to the local repo.

GitHub Desktop

GitHub Desktop gives you a tremendous amount of information on one screen:

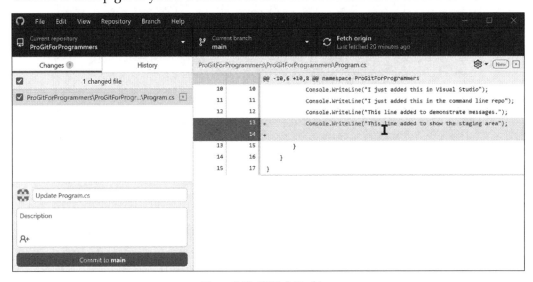

Figure 3.10: GitHub Desktop

On the top row, you can see the name of the repository and the current branch. In the window on the upper left, you can see that one file changed, and which file that is. On the right, you can see the actual change.

Finally, on the lower left, you can put in your message and commit your file.

As soon as you commit, the page is cleared and a new button appears to allow you to push the changes to the server.

Local and remote repositories

The third and fourth areas for Git are the local and remote repositories. We've covered this in the previous chapter so all I'll repeat here is that commit puts your files into the *local* repository and push sends your commit from your local repository to the remote one.

While I believe in committing frequently, you'll want to put in a few commits before you push. This will give you the opportunity to combine similar commits as we'll see in *Chapter 6, Interactive Rebasing* on interactive rebase.

The stash

The fifth and final area for Git is the stash. The stash, as it sounds, is a place to stash away files that you've modified but don't want to commit or lose when changing branches. We'll see more of this just below, when we discuss branching.

Branches

Using branches is critical to working with Git, not to mention to the success of your project. The idea is this: you have a "main" branch that you'll do your releases from. Each time code is added to the main branch it is checked and reviewed so that the main branch stays as clean as possible.

When you want to work on a bug or a feature, you create a new branch (often called a feature branch). This creates a copy of the code that is currently in the main branch. You can work on your feature branch without affecting the main branch at all. Once you are done, and all is working, you can then "merge" your feature branch into the main branch:

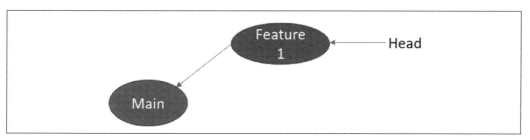

Figure 3.11: First feature branch

Notice that there is a pointer named **Head**. This points to whatever is in your work area. In this case, we've branched to **Feature 1** and **Head** shows that the code for that feature branch is now in our work area.

That is a pretty good simplification of branching but there is a good deal more to it. First, let's see how to do it. Until now, all your code has been on the Main branch – a bad practice. We should have created a feature branch before doing any coding. That said, we can do so now.

From the command line, you simply check out Main (putting whatever is at the tip of Main into your work area. The tip means the most recent commit). Once you are in Main you will `pull` from the remote repository to get the very latest version of Main. You are now ready to create your first branch. The sequence of commands looks like this:

```
) git checkout main
Switched to branch 'main'
Your branch is up to date with 'origin/main'.
SESA560987@DESKTOP-D21661F  ▶  C:\GitHub\CommandLine\ProGitForProgrammers  〉 ⌕ main ≡
) git pull
Already up to date.
SESA560987@DESKTOP-D21661F  ▶  C:\GitHub\CommandLine\ProGitForProgrammers  〉 ⌕ main ≡
) git branch Calculator
SESA560987@DESKTOP-D21661F  ▶  C:\GitHub\CommandLine\ProGitForProgrammers  〉 ⌕ main ≡
) git checkout Calculator
Switched to branch 'Calculator'
SESA560987@DESKTOP-D21661F  ▶  C:\GitHub\CommandLine\ProGitForProgrammers  〉 ⌕ Calculator ⇵
```

Figure 3.12: Creating branch on command line

Note that creating the branch `Calculator` did not check it out; you must do that as a separate step. However, if you use the -b flag, then you can create the branch and check it out at the same time:

```
git checkout -b Calculator
```

In either case, the new branch is in the work area. But what is in that branch? Because that branch was created from main, and we've not changed anything yet, the new branch is identical to the main branch. From here they will diverge. As you add code, it will be in the new branch (`Calculator`) but not in the main one.

Before we look at that in depth, let's create branches for the Visual Studio user and for the GitHub Desktop user.

The easiest way to do this (and the least confusing) is to open Windows Explorer and navigate to the `VisualStudio` folder (in my case, **GitHub | VisualStudio | ProGitForProgrammers | ProGitForProgrammers**). In that folder is a `.sln` file, which I will double-click on, opening Visual Studio. (This book was originally named Pro Git For Programmers and you will see that name in the code quite a bit.)

 Don't be confused between the VisualStudio folder (which we are using to demonstrate Git in Visual Studio) and the program itself, which we use to modify the code in all three places (CommandLine, GitHubDesktop, and VisualStudio).

It might be less confusing if you think of these as three separate programmers, each one on their own computer (mimicked here by using separate directories). Each programmer has a main branch and each one is now branching off for their own work.

We want to put this on a branch as well, and to reduce confusion we'll call this branch Book. To create the branch, click on the **Git** menu and select **New Branch**. Give the new branch the name Book, and press **Create**:

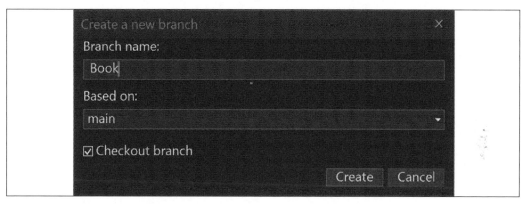

Figure 3.13: Creating a new branch in Visual Studio

When you do, a window will open on the left that lists the branches for this repository and Book will be in bold indicating that it is the current branch:

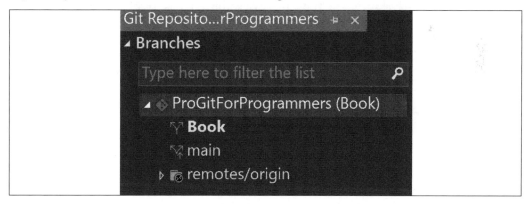

Figure 3.14: Branches menu in Visual Studio

Two of the users have now branched off of main. Let's use GitHub Desktop to create a third branch. Open the program and click on the menu choice **Repository**. On that menu click on **Show In Explorer** and make sure you are in the path C:\GitHub\ GitHubDesktop\ProGitForProgrammers.

It should indicate that you have one pull from the origin (the server) and have a button that says **Pull Origin**. Go ahead and click that button. That brings down the latest version of **Main**. You now should see that the button says **Push Origin** – that's to push up to the server the two commits that are now sitting in this directory.

To create your new branch, click on the **Branch** menu choice and select **New Branch**. It will prompt you for the name of your new branch. Enter Movie and click **Create**. The interface now asks if you want to publish your branch. Publishing in GitHub Desktop simply means uploading it for the first time. Let's hold off on that and first make some commits.

Programmer 1 (CommandLine) and calculator

Open Visual Studio in the CommandLine directory path. In the Solution Explorer, you should see Program.cs, which has five WriteLine statements. Add a new class named Calculator and set it to public:

```
namespace ProGitForProgrammers
{
    public class Calculator
    {
    }
}
```

Normally we would not create a commit after so little work, but for this book, to make simple examples, we'll be doing a great deal of committing. Return to the command line and get the status. It will tell you that you have one untracked file. Git has recognized that there is a file in the directory that it knows nothing about. Our next step is to add it to Git:

```
git add .
```

By using the dot, the add command will add any modified or new files to the staging area. You can then commit the new file just by writing:

```
git commit -m "Add calculator class"
```

If you write `git status` now, Git will tell you that you are on the branch `Calculator`, that you have nothing to commit, and that your working tree is clean.

We're going to talk about the `log` command in detail in *Chapter 9, Using the Log*, but for now, let's just use it to see our commit and the message that went with it:

```
git log --oneline
```

This will display all of your commits, one per line:

```
> git log --oneline
e5c4db9 (HEAD -> Calculator) Add calculator class
b00ca09 (origin/main, origin/HEAD, main, featureOne) Demonstrating the
staging area
4ac9d40 Add a line to program to indicate why it was added
ef16f81 Add writeline indicating we are in command line
d418600 Add informative WriteLine
a3f085e First commit -- from command line
a5798e1 Initial commit
```

The seven-digit hexadecimal identifier is the "short ID" and is enough to uniquely identify each commit. They are listed in newest-to-oldest order. Our most recent commit says:

```
e5c4db9 (HEAD -> Calculator) Add calculator class
```

This tells you that your Head pointer is pointing to your **Calculator** branch (that is, what is in your working area right now is the **Calculator** branch) and it displays the message we added for that commit. Graphically, it might look like this:

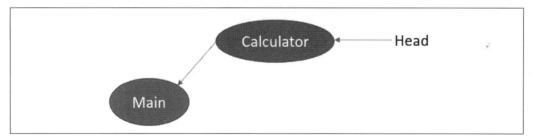

Figure 3.15: Head pointer

Notice that the arrow runs from **Calculator** to **Main**. Each commit points to its parent.

Pushing the new branch

We can push this commit up to the server, but the server doesn't know about this branch. When we enter `git push`, we get back this message:

```
> git push
fatal: The current branch Calculator has no upstream branch.
To push the current branch and set the remote as upstream, use

    git push --set-upstream origin Calculator
```

It is saying that it could not proceed (`fatal`) because the current branch (which is `Calculator`) does not correspond to a branch on the server. Wonderfully, however, it gives us the command line to use. Just copy the command and paste it at the prompt and hit *Enter*. Hey presto! You've pushed your branch up to the server:

```
> git push
fatal: The current branch Calculator has no upstream branch.
To push the current branch and set the remote as upstream, use

    git push --set-upstream origin Calculator

SESA560987@DESKTOP-D21661F ▶ C:\GitHub\CommandLine\ProGitForProgrammers ▶ ⑂ Calculator ≢
> git push --set-upstream origin Calculator
Enumerating objects: 37, done.
Counting objects: 100% (37/37), done.
Delta compression using up to 16 threads
Compressing objects: 100% (37/37), done.
Writing objects: 100% (37/37), 6.94 KiB | 710.00 KiB/s, done.
Total 37 (delta 19), reused 4 (delta 0), pack-reused 0
remote: Resolving deltas: 100% (19/19), done.
remote:
remote: Create a pull request for 'Calculator' on GitHub by visiting:
remote:      https://github.com/JesseLiberty/ProGitForProgrammers/pull/new/Calculator
remote:
To github.com:JesseLiberty/ProGitForProgrammers.git
 * [new branch]      Calculator → Calculator
Branch 'Calculator' set up to track remote branch 'Calculator' from 'origin'.
```

Figure 3.16: Pushing to the server

For now, you can ignore all the other messages; what you care about is the last two lines, indicating that you now have a branch, `Calculator`, on the server, and that on the server it is also called `Calculator`.

Note that from now on, when pushing commits on the `Calculator` branch, you won't have to use that line; you'll just be able to write `git push`.

Examining origin

Let's go to GitHub and examine our new branch. Sign in and select the ProGitForProgrammers repository:

Figure 3.17: Repository on server

So, where is our calculator folder? Notice the button in the upper left that says **main**. Drop that down and choose **Calculator** – which will display the contents of the Calculator branch:

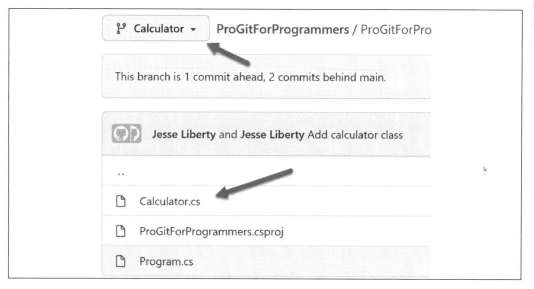

Figure 3.18: Calculator branch on server

You can see that the Calculator branch *does* have the expected file.

Adding commits to a branch

Let's add another commit to our branch. Return to Visual Studio and give our `Calculator` class an add method:

```
public int Add (int left, int right)
{
    return left + right;
}
```

Again, just to have lots of commits, let's commit this. The easiest way is to combine the add and the commit and to add a message on a single line:

```
git commit -a -m "Add the add method"
```

To see that this was in fact committed, run the `log` command again:

```
> git log --oneline
4f9817b (HEAD → Calculator) Add the add method
e5c4db9 (origin/Calculator) Add calculator class
b00ca09 (origin/main, origin/HEAD, main, featureOne) Demonstrating the staging area
4ac9d40 Add a line to program to indicate why it was added
ef16f81 Add writeline indicating we are in command line
d418600 Add informative WriteLine
a3f085e First commit -- from command line
a5798e1 Initial commit
```

Figure 3.19: Tracking HEAD

If you study this for a moment, not only will you see that our commit worked (it is the first one listed) but also that we have various pointers. On the first line, we see that HEAD is pointing to our `Calculator` branch. Good enough.

The second line indicates that the `Calculator` branch on origin (GitHub) is pointing to the previous commit. We have one commit to push.

The third line shows us that main on origin, HEAD on origin, the main branch, and the `featureOne` branch are all pointing to the third most recent commit. All this is fine. We expect `Calculator` to have diverged from main, and we can push our commit if we like, or we can wait until we have a few of them.

The Book branch – Git within Visual Studio

Let's turn our attention to the Visual Studio programmer. You will remember that this takes place in the `VisualStudio` folder. Let's open Visual Studio in that directory, and note that in the upper right, it says **1 outgoing** – this indicates that we have a commit to push. Click on it and Visual Studio opens two more windows.

One shows that Book is the current branch (see above) and the other shows the history of your commits (not unlike log).

There is a section in the middle window that shows what was committed locally and what awaits commitment in the outgoing section. Also note that Book and main are indicated as outgoing:

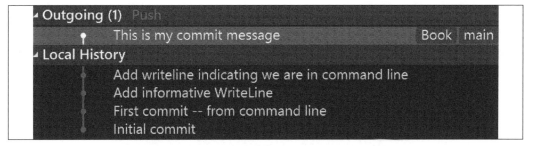

Figure 3.20: Commitments window Visual Studio

To push these commits find the tiny up arrow in the upper-right corner (magnified here):

Figure 3.21: Link to push files on Visual Studio

Let's create a Book class. The process is similar to the creation of the Calculator class above. Right-click on the project and choose **Add | Class**. Name your new class "Book". Make your Book class public and give it three properties:

```
0 references | 0 authors, 0 changes
public class Book
{
    0 references | 0 authors, 0 changes
    public string Title {get; set;}
    0 references | 0 authors, 0 changes
    public List<string> Authors {get; set;}

    0 references | 0 authors, 0 changes
    public DateTime PublicationDate {get; set;}
}
```

Figure 3.22: New Book class

Let's commit this. To do so either click on the **Git** menu choice and choose **Commit or Stash**, or click on the pencil at the bottom of the screen. Either way, you will be brought to the commit screen. Notice that it says **1 outgoing**. Click on the up arrow. That will push our previous commit. You will get back a message saying that you have successfully pushed Book to origin.

Committing with GitHub Desktop

Open Visual Studio in the GitHubDesktop directory. Here we will create the Movie class and give it two properties: Title and a collection of people (which we will represent as strings to keep things simple):

```
0 references | 0 authors, 0 changes
public class Movie
{
    0 references | 0 authors, 0 changes
    public string Title {get; set;}
    0 references | 0 authors, 0 changes
    public List<string> Actors {get; set;}
}
```

Figure 3.23: Movie class

Now open GitHub Desktop. It recognizes and displays the changes (with deleted lines in red and new lines in green). It also offers you the opportunity to check in the new changes:

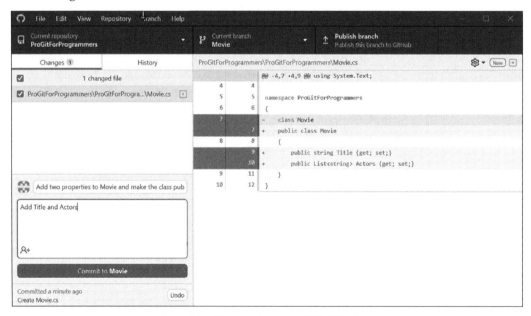

Figure 3.24: Changes shown in GitHub Desktop

You can see the changes highlighted above, in *Figure 3.24.*

Status

You can see that the GUIs make the work easier, but that the command line makes the steps more explicit. Our repository looks like this (conceptually):

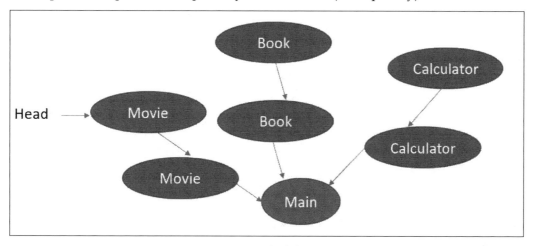

Figure 3.25: Multiple branches

What's on origin?

It's important to remember that this map of commits only applies to the local repository. What is on the remote repository may or may not be the same for any given branch depending on whether you've pushed all your commits. In *Chapter 6, Interactive Rebasing*, we'll review why you might want to hold on to a number of commits before pushing them (in short, you will have the ability to combine commits to reduce the number of commits a reviewer must slog through).

Adding more commits

We'd like to add a number of commits so that we can review their history and to set us up for future chapters. To do so, we'll want to work on the CommandLine project. You can, as we have done already, open Windows Explorer and navigate to the appropriate directory, and then double-click on `ProGitForProgrammers.sln`. An alternative is to open Visual Studio from anywhere and then choose **File | Recent Projects and Solutions**, and click on the one you want, in this case, `ProGitForProgrammers (C:\GitHub\CommandLine\ProGitForProgrammers)`.

Visual Studio will open to the Calculator folder. Just to triple-check that you are in the right place, right-click on the project and select **Open Folder In File Explorer**. You should see a Windows Explorer window open in the expected folder (no matter which folder you started out in). Let's add a Subtract method:

```
public int Add (int left, int right)
{
    return left + right;
}
public int Subtract (int left, int right)
{
    return left - right;
}
```

While we normally wouldn't commit for such a small change, let's go ahead now and turn to the command line. As always we start with a git status:

```
> git status
On branch Calculator
Your branch is ahead of 'origin/Calculator' by 1 commit.
  (use "git push" to publish your local commits)

Changes not staged for commit:
  (use "git add <file> ... " to update what will be committed)
  (use "git restore <file> ... " to discard changes in working directory)
        modified:   ProGitForProgrammers/ProGitForProgrammers/Calculator.cs

no changes added to commit (use "git add" and/or "git commit -a")
```

Figure 3.26: git status

Let's read through this carefully. The first line after git status confirms that you are on the Calculator branch. Next comes a notice that you are ahead of origin/Calculator by one commit. That means that you didn't push your last commit (and this is true).

Next comes a paragraph telling you that Calculator.cs has been modified and gives you a couple of commands you might want to use in this context. Let's use the add command to place our modified file in the index.

Rather than typing the name of the modified file, we'll use a period (.) to indicate that we want everything changed in the working directory (in this case, just the one file):

```
git add .
```

Git makes no real acknowledgment, but if you request the status, you'll find that the modified file is now a different color (on most setups) and that the message is slightly different, as you now have that modified file in the index:

```
> git status
On branch Calculator
Your branch is ahead of 'origin/Calculator' by 1 commit.
  (use "git push" to publish your local commits)

Changes to be committed:
  (use "git restore --staged <file>..." to unstage)
        modified:   ProGitForProgrammers/ProGitForProgrammers/Calculator.cs
```

Figure 3.27: Modified files in git status

Git helpfully gives you a command to unstage your files if you choose to do so. Be careful with the restore command, however. If you use it as shown with the --staged flag you will unstage your file, but if you leave out the flag you will restore your file to your last commit, **losing all the work you've done in the interim**.

In our case, we want to commit that change, and so we will enter:

```
git commit -m "Add subtract method"
```

Notice that we don't need the -a flag as the files we want to commit have already been added to the index.

Add a multiply method and commit it. Next, add an integer division method and commit that as well:

```
public int Add(int left, int right)
{
    return left + right;
}
public int Subtract(int left, int right)
{
    return left - right;
}

public int Multiply(int left, int right)
{
    return left * right;
}

public int Divide(int left, int right)
{
    return left / right;
}
```

Examining your commits

Enter the log command:

```
git log -oneline
```

```
> git log --oneline
8434d6d (HEAD -> Calculator) Add integer division method
b03ce53 Add multiply method
4f9817b Add the add method
e5c4db9 (origin/Calculator) Add calculator class
```

Figure 3.28: log command

Again, examine the output carefully. The first line tells you that HEAD is pointing to the Calculator branch, as we would expect. Below that are a couple of commits and then you see a line that indicates that Calculator on origin is only up to commit e5c4db9 (the one where the message is Add calculator class).

Is that right? There are a couple of ways to tell. The easiest is to go to GitHub and see if the Calculator class has what this indicates:

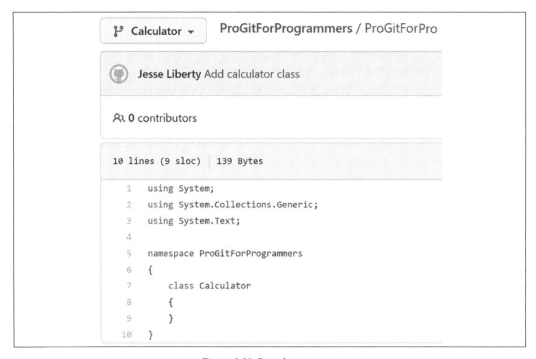

Figure 3.29: Branch on server

Notice in the upper left that we are on the `Calculator` branch. Now drill down to the code. What you see is only the class in its initial state. This is consistent with what the log showed.

There is one more way to tell. Return to Visual Studio and click on the **3** next to the up arrow on the right side of the very bottom of the application:

Figure 3.30: Accessing history on Visual Studio

When you do, a window will open that shows your local history and the "outgoing" files – that is, the ones you've not yet pushed:

▲ Outgoing (3) Push					
Add integer division method	Calculator	Jesse...	2/8/2...	8434d.
Add multiply method		Jesse...	2/8/2...	b03ce.
Add the add method		Jesse...	2/7/2...	4f981.
▲ Local History					
Add calculator class		Jesse...	2/7/2...	e5c4d.
Demonstrating the staging area	featureOne main	Jesse...	2/7/2...	b00ca.
Add a line to program to indicate why it was added		Jesse...	2/3/2...	4ac9d.
Add writeline indicating we are in command line		Jesse...	2/2/2...	ef16f8.
Add informative WriteLine		Jesse...	2/2/2...	d4186.
First commit -- from command line		Jesse...	2/1/2...	a3f08.
Initial commit		Jesse...	2/1/2...	a5798.

Figure 3.31: History in Visual Studio

Again, this is consistent with what `log` has shown.

Summary

In this chapter, you have learned about the crucial "five places" for Git: the work area, the index, the local repository, the remote repository, and the stash. You have seen how to use each of these and how they work together.

Each concept was illustrated with both code and screenshots, and every Git action was illustrated in the command line, Visual Studio, and GitHub Desktop.

Finally, you have learned about creating branches, committing code, and how to move commits from the work area to the repository and from the repository to the remote repository.

Challenge

Create a private repository on GitHub named Contacts, and then clone that repository down to a folder on your disk. Using the command line, create a feature branch named Person and in that feature branch, create a person object with their name, age, and social security number. Create commits as you add each attribute. Review the log to see what you've created and then add these commits to the remote repository.

Answer

There is no one right way to do this, but we'll walk through a likely answer.

Task #1 – create a private repository on GitHub named Contacts. To do this, open a browser to Github.com and navigate to your repository page. Click on **New** and fill in the fields as shown here:

Figure 3.32: New repo on server

Notice that I've marked the repository as private. Click the **Create Repository** button.

Task #2 – clone that repository down to a folder on your disk.

On the same GitHub page, click on **Code** and click on the clipboard to copy the HTTPS or SSH path (if you have SSH you'll know it, otherwise choose HTTPS):

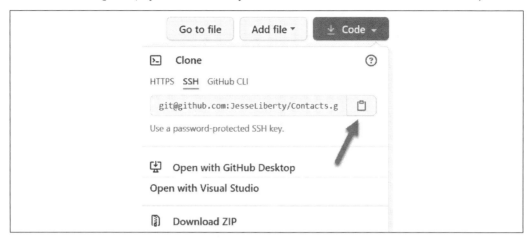

Figure 3.33: Copy address from server

Open the command line where you want your cloned repo and type:

```
git clone
```

and paste in the link you just copied:

```
git clone git@github.com:JesseLiberty/Contacts.git
```

You should see something like this:

```
SESA560987@DESKTOP-D21661F ▶ C:\GitHub
) git clone git@github.com:JesseLiberty/Contacts.git
Cloning into 'Contacts'...
remote: Enumerating objects: 5, done.
remote: Counting objects: 100% (5/5), done.
remote: Compressing objects: 100% (4/4), done.
remote: Total 5 (delta 0), reused 0 (delta 0), pack-reused 0
Receiving objects: 100% (5/5), done.
SESA560987@DESKTOP-D21661F ▶ C:\GitHub
) cd Contacts
SESA560987@DESKTOP-D21661F ▶ C:\GitHub\Contacts ⟩ ⌥ main ≡ ⟩
```

Figure 3.34: Cloning from server to local repo

This indicates that you have cloned Contacts from GitHub into a directory named Contacts and then you have changed to that directory.

Task #3 – using the command line, create a feature branch named Person.

To create a feature branch, we'll use the branch command and the checkout command (or the cb alias):

```
> git branch person
SESA560987@DESKTOP-D21661F ▶ C:\GitHub\Contacts ⟩ ⎇ main ≡
> git checkout person
Switched to branch 'person'
SESA560987@DESKTOP-D21661F ▶ C:\GitHub\Contacts ⟩ ⎇ person ≢
```

Figure 3.35: Creating a branch

Task #4 – in that feature branch, create a person object with their name, age, and social security number. Create commits as you add each attribute.

For this I created my project (Contacts) and then within a folder, I added the Person class:

Figure 3.36: Adding the Person class

Creating the class was intentionally trivial:

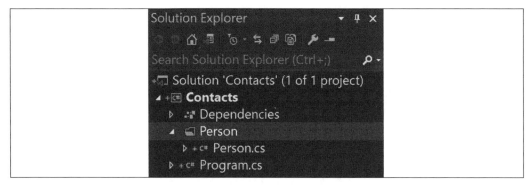

```
namespace Contacts.Person
{
    0 references | 0 authors, 0 changes
    public class Person
    {
        0 references | 0 authors, 0 changes
        public string Name {get; set;}
        0 references | 0 authors, 0 changes
        public double Age {get; set;}
        0 references | 0 authors, 0 changes
        public string SSN {get; set;}
    }
}
```

Figure 3.37: Person properties

I then returned to the command line to check in these changes.

Remember to save your file before each commit or the command line will tell you that there is nothing to commit.

Task #5 – review the log to see what you've created:

```
> git log --oneline
11551f3 (HEAD -> person) Added SSN
49bd5de Added age
f5ee20b Added name
1174250 (origin/main, origin/HEAD, main) Initial commit
```

Figure 3.38: Examining the log

Task #6 – add these commits to the remote repository.

We'll try to push, but the remote repository won't have heard of our branch. Fortunately, Git tells us what to do:

```
> git push
fatal: The current branch person has no upstream branch.
To push the current branch and set the remote as upstream, use

    git push --set-upstream origin person

SESA560987@DESKTOP-D21661F  C:\GitHub\Contacts   person ≢
>  git push --set-upstream origin person
Enumerating objects: 22, done.
Counting objects: 100% (22/22), done.
Delta compression using up to 16 threads
Compressing objects: 100% (18/18), done.
Writing objects: 100% (21/21), 2.34 KiB | 480.00 KiB/s, done.
Total 21 (delta 4), reused 0 (delta 0), pack-reused 0
remote: Resolving deltas: 100% (4/4), done.
remote:
remote: Create a pull request for 'person' on GitHub by visiting:
remote:       https://github.com/JesseLiberty/Contacts/pull/new/person
remote:
To github.com:JesseLiberty/Contacts.git
 * [new branch]      person -> person
Branch 'person' set up to track remote branch 'person' from 'origin'.
SESA560987@DESKTOP-D21661F  C:\GitHub\Contacts   person ≡
```

Figure 3.39: Pushing to server

At this point, you have a local and remote repository named Contacts and a branch named Person. On the branch named Person you have code for a skeleton class named Person. A quick review of GitHub shows that main does not have a Person object (or class, or folder):

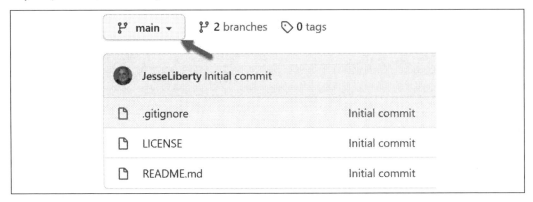

Figure 3.40: Branches on origin

But the Person branch does:

Figure 3.41: Person branch on origin

As you can see, the Person branch does have the expected code.

4

Merging, Pull Requests, and Handling Merge Conflicts

In this chapter, you will see how to merge branches, using different types of merges. You will also see how to handle merge conflicts and tools to make managing conflicts easier. You will learn about pull requests and the difference between a fast-forward merge and a "true" merge.

In this chapter, you will learn:

- How to push a commit to the server
- How to manage your commits with the command line, Visual Studio, and GitHub Desktop
- How to merge into the main branch
- What a pull request is
- What merge conflicts are and how to resolve them
- What a fast-forward merge is
- What a true merge is

Let's start with an overview of merging.

Merging overview

If you are on a feature branch, and the feature is sufficiently complete and tested, you will want to merge your branch back into the main branch. Some organizations let you simply merge, others (most?) require that you create a **Pull Request (PR)**. A **PR** says, essentially, "Please examine my code and if you think it is right, merge it into the main branch."

Having a second (or third) set of eyes on your code before merging can save a lot of headaches later on (see *Chapter 12, Fixing Mistakes (Undo)*, on fixing mistakes).

Often, if you've been careful (see below) you will merge without a problem. From time to time, however, you will run into the dreaded merge conflict. You'll see below a couple ways to handle that conflict.

Book

You will remember from the previous chapter that we have a directory, `C:\GitHub\ VisualStudio\ProGitForProgrammers`, that is the home of the Books application and that we've been editing in Visual Studio. Of course, we don't have to manage it in Visual Studio; we can use any of our tools. For example, I can open the terminal and change directories to the Books app:

```
SESA560987@DESKTOP-D21661F  C:\GitHub\VisualStudio\ProGitForProgrammers   Book ↑1
> _
```

Figure 4.1: Opening the terminal

Notice that it says I have one commit to push (as indicated by the up-pointing arrow followed by the 1). I must have forgotten to do so the last time I was working with this code. I don't want to just push it, however — who knows what's in there? There are a few ways to find out.

What's in that push?

From the command line, we can use the `git show` command:

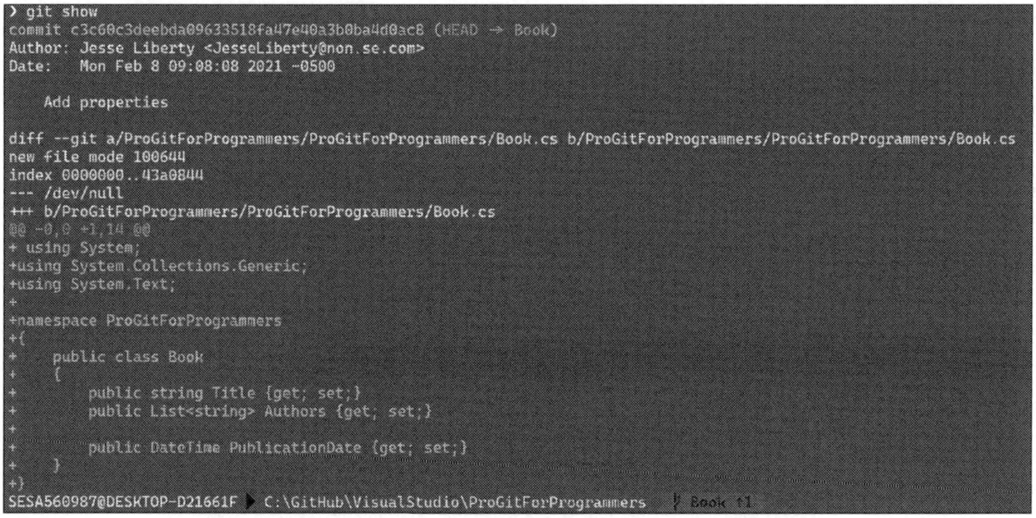

```
> git show
commit c3c60c3deebda09633518fa47e40a3b0ba4d0ac8 (HEAD -> Book)
Author: Jesse Liberty <JesseLiberty@non.se.com>
Date:   Mon Feb 8 09:08:08 2021 -0500

    Add properties

diff --git a/ProGitForProgrammers/ProGitForProgrammers/Book.cs b/ProGitForProgrammers/ProGitForProgrammers/Book.cs
new file mode 100644
index 0000000..43a0844
--- /dev/null
+++ b/ProGitForProgrammers/ProGitForProgrammers/Book.cs
@@ -0,0 +1,14 @@
+ using System;
+using System.Collections.Generic;
+using System.Text;
+
+namespace ProGitForProgrammers
+{
+    public class Book
+    {
+        public string Title {get; set;}
+        public List<string> Authors {get; set;}
+
+        public DateTime PublicationDate {get; set;}
+    }
+}
SESA560987@DESKTOP-D21661F   C:\GitHub\VisualStudio\ProGitForProgrammers    Book ±1
```

Figure 4.2: Examining the push

There's a lot of information here. First, we see the author and the date. Then we see the message that was attached to this commit (Add properties). Next, Git does a diff (difference) between Book.cs and Book.cs naming the first one **a** and the second **b**. The one labeled **a** is Book.cs before this commit, the one labeled **b** is the new contents in this commit.

You may have noticed the line that says /dev/null. This indicates that a file is being compared against nothing, and thus everything is new.

The next line shows that /dev/null is being compared against file **b** (the new Book.cs file):

```
diff --git a/ProGitForProgrammers/ProGitForProgrammers/Bo
new file mode 100644
index 0000000..43a0844
--- /dev/null
+++ b/ProGitForProgrammers/ProGitForProgrammers/Book.cs
```

Figure 4.3: Comparing against dev/null

What follows are the changes. Deletions will be marked in red, modifications in green, and new code in yellow. (This display and these colors may depend on which shell you are using.) We see here that three using statements, a namespace, and the class Book were all added in this commit. Before we push it, let's see what we can learn in Visual Studio.

Visual Studio

Opening the same directory in Visual Studio and going to the Git view reveals, as we would expect, that we have one commit to push (outgoing):

Figure 4.4: Visual Studio showing one file to push

Before we push, let's see what's in that push. Clicking on **1 outgoing** opens two windows. The **Branches** window shows us which branch we are on (**Book**):

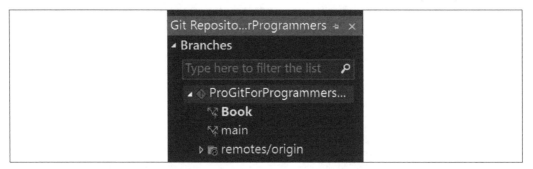

Figure 4.5: Visual Studio showing contents of the local repository

The middle panel has the really cool info. It tells you the local (as opposed to origin) history of your branches:

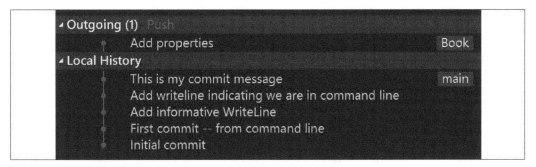

Figure 4.6: Visual Studio showing commit history

We can see that **main** has five commits (reading newest to oldest) and that preceding the newest commit in **main**, we have an outgoing commit on the **Book** branch, whose message is **Add properties**. This is consistent with what we saw at the command line.

We can go further, and return to **Solution Explorer**. Because there is more to see in Program.cs (rather than Book.cs), right-click on Program.cs and choose **Git** and then **History**. That opens the **History** page for Program.cs:

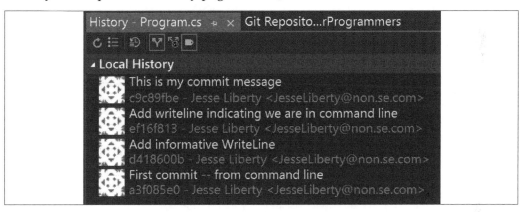

Figure 4.7: Visual Studio showing the history of Program.cs

 Note that if we registered a user with an image, that image would be shown on the extreme left.

Here we see the four commits. We can compare them by right-clicking on, for example, the first one and choosing **Compare with previous**. Two windows open. On the left, you have the older commit, on the right the newer. We can see that in the newer commit one line was added, which is shown in Visual Studio with green highlighting:

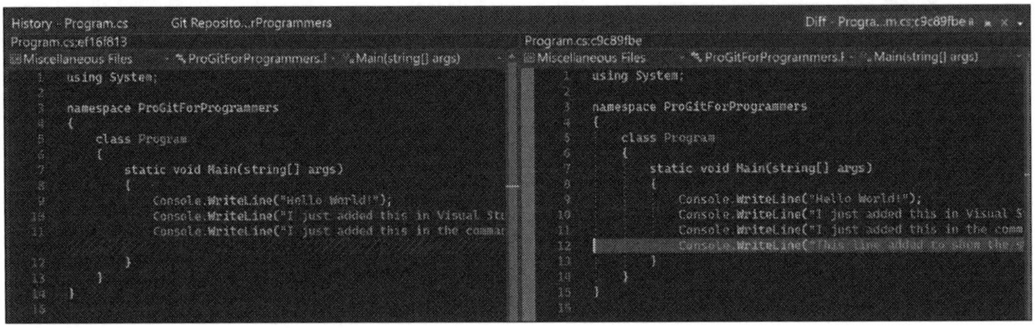

Figure 4.8: Side-by-side comparison

You can see that Visual Studio can give you a graphic representation of the same information you might get from the command line.

Details, details

Let's close all these history windows and go back to the list of outgoing and local history. Under **Outgoing**, we see **Add properties**. Right-click on that line and a window will open on the right. You'll see the commit ID (ID) along with the name of the committer, the date, and so forth. You'll also see the message and then you'll see a list of which files were changed (in this case, **Book.cs**):

Figure 4.9: Visual Studio showing which files have changed for a commit

We want to know what changed in Book.cs. To do this, right-click on Book.cs and choose **View History**. The single commit will come up in the middle window. Double-click on that and you'll see the Book class that is being added by this commit.

GitHub Desktop

We can open GitHub Desktop to the same directory. Click on **File** and choose **Add local repository...**:

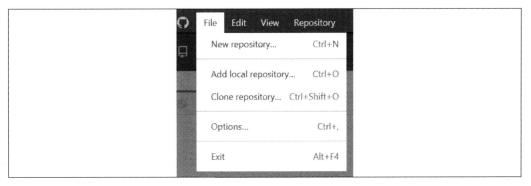

Figure 4.10: Opening GitHub Desktop

The next step is to tell GitHub Desktop where that repository is. A dialog opens and you can either enter the local path by hand, or you can click **Choose...**, which will bring you to a Windows Explorer window where you can pick the appropriate directory. Once that is all set, click **Add repository**:

Figure 4.11: Adding a local repository

You'll now be brought to the main page. Notice that we are still in the repository **ProGitForProgrammers**, but on the **Book** branch, and that it knows we have one commit to push. It also offers a handy **Push origin** button with an explanation that pressing that button will push the commit to the origin (the server; your repository on GitHub):

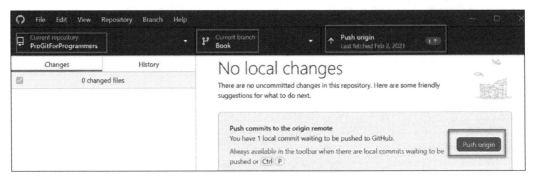

Figure 4.12: GitHub Desktop information bar

Once again, we want to know what we are pushing. No problem, just click **History** and you'll see the history of commits and the changes for whichever commit you highlight:

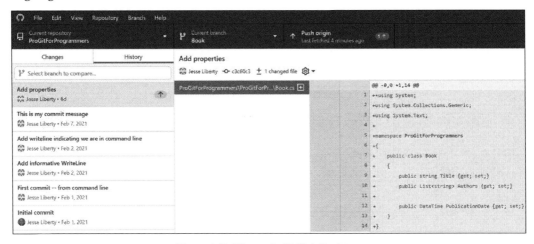

Figure 4.13: History in GitHub Desktop

Now that we've seen the various ways the command line, Visual Studio, and GitHub Desktop manage the commit, it is time to get the commit to the server.

Push it already

Let's return to the command line and push the commit we've been examining:

```
> git push
Enumerating objects: 7, done.
Counting objects: 100% (7/7), done.
Delta compression using up to 16 threads
Compressing objects: 100% (5/5), done.
Writing objects: 100% (5/5), 601 bytes | 300.00 KiB/s, done.
Total 5 (delta 2), reused 0 (delta 0), pack-reused 0
remote: Resolving deltas: 100% (2/2), completed with 2 local objects.
To github.com:JesseLiberty/ProGitForProgrammers.git
   c9c89fb..c3c60c3  Book -> Book
```

Figure 4.14: Pushing from the command line

If you go to Visual Studio now, it should say **0 outgoing** as you've pushed the one that was waiting. Similarly, GitHub Desktop will have changed its button from **Push Origin** to **Create Pull Request** – the likely next thing to do.

Now that we have the Book branch sorted, it is (finally!) time to merge it into **main**.

Visual Studio

Our goal is to merge Book back into main. To do this in Visual Studio, just click on **Git** and then on **Manage Branches**. Your **Branches** window will open. Right-click on **main** and choose **Checkout**. You are now ready to merge Book into main, which you'll see in the right-click (context) menu as well:

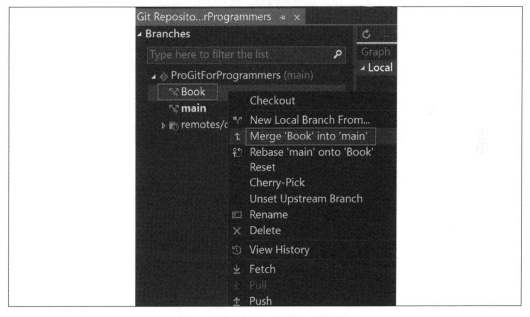

Figure 4.15: Merging in Visual Studio

The trick is, while main is checked out, right-click on **Book** and you'll see the option to make the merge.

Merge conflicts

Let's turn to the command line and do a pull as our branch has diverged from the origin. When we do, we're told that there is a merge conflict in `Program.cs` and that the merge has failed. Git tells you to fix the conflicts and then commit the result. This is unusual, to get a merge conflict on a pull, but as you can see, it does happen. Let's handle this conflict and then set up a more typical situation:

```
> git pull
Auto-merging ProGitForProgrammers/ProGitForProgrammers/Program.cs
CONFLICT (content): Merge conflict in ProGitForProgrammers/ProGitForProgrammers/Program.cs
Automatic merge failed; fix conflicts and then commit the result.
SESA560987@DESKTOP-D21661F ▶ C:\GitHub\VisualStudio\ProGitForProgrammers ⑂ main ↑1 ↓4 +0 ~0 -0 !1
```

Figure 4.16: A merge conflict

There are a few ways to handle any merge, but the easiest is to use a merge tool. I use KDiff3 (`https://sourceforge.net/projects/kdiff3/`). Since I use this a lot, I have put it into my config file:

```
git config --edit --global
```

```
[merge]
        tool = kdiff3
[mergetool]
        prompt = false
        keepBackup = false
        keepTemporaries = false
[mergetool "kdiff3"]
        path =   c:kdiff3\\kdiff3
```

Figure 4.17: Reviewing the configuration file

This sets up KDiff3 as my merge tool and tells Git where to find it. One of the things I like most about KDiff is that it will often fix the problem for you.

To invoke it, all I need to write is:

```
git mergetool
```

and it opens KDiff to the conflict.

Here it found two problems and was able to fix one:

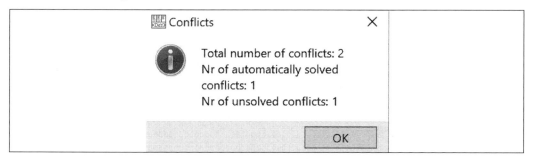

Figure 4.18: KDiff automatically solves one conflict

It then brings us to a window with multiple panes. The panes on top show you the conflict:

Figure 4.19: Conflicts as shown in KDiff

You can see on the left side (**Local**) that we have one line whereas on the right side (**Remote**) we have two lines. Clearly, someone else has edited this file that we edited and now Git doesn't know what to do.

In the bottom pane is code to provide context and then a highlighted line where your choice of which line(s) to place there is shown:

```
Output: C:\GitHub\VisualStudio\ProGitForProgrammers\ProGitForProgrammers\ProGitForProgrammers\Program.cs
using System;

namespace ProGitForProgrammers
{
    class Program
    {
        static void Main(string[] args)
        {
            Console.WriteLine("Hello World!");
            Console.WriteLine("I just added this in Visual Studio");
            Console.WriteLine("I just added this in the command line repo");
<Merge Conflict>
            Console.WriteLine("This line added to show the staging area");
```

Figure 4.20: KDiff provides context for your merge

When you right-click on that line, you are given a choice to pick the left window (window A), the right window (window B), or both (and you can choose the order they are added in):

```
class Program
{
    static void Main(string[] args)
    {
        Console.WriteLine("Hello World!");
        Console.WriteLine("I just added this
        Console.WriteLine("I just added this
rge Conflict>
        Console.Wr  ᴀ  Select Line(s) From A     Ctrl+1
                    ʙ  Select Line(s) From B     Ctrl+2
```

Figure 4.21: KDiff asking which version should be placed

Once you are done, save the file and close KDiff. <poof\> No more conflict. Git now shows you the changes you made that should now be committed:

```
On branch main
Your branch and 'origin/main' have diverged,
and have 1 and 4 different commits each, respectively.
  (use "git pull" to merge the remote branch into yours)

All conflicts fixed but you are still merging.
  (use "git commit" to conclude merge)

Changes to be committed:
        modified:   ProGitForProgrammers/ProGitForProgrammers/Program.cs
```

Figure 4.22: Console indicating that the conflicts have been resolved

You can now add that file and commit it, and then push it up to the origin:

```
> git add .
SESA560987@DESKTOP-D21661F ▸ C:\GitHub\VisualStudio\ProGitForProgrammers    ⑂ main ↑1 ↓4
> git commit
[main 9de1dc1] Merge branch 'main' of github.com:JesseLiberty/ProGitForProgrammers
SESA560987@DESKTOP-D21661F ▸ C:\GitHub\VisualStudio\ProGitForProgrammers    ⑂ main ↑2
> git push
Enumerating objects: 1, done.
Counting objects: 100% (1/1), done.
Writing objects: 100% (1/1), 252 bytes | 252.00 KiB/s, done.
Total 1 (delta 0), reused 0 (delta 0), pack-reused 0
To github.com:JesseLiberty/ProGitForProgrammers.git
   8543803..9de1dc1  main -> main
SESA560987@DESKTOP-D21661F ▸ C:\GitHub\VisualStudio\ProGitForProgrammers    ⑂ main ≡
```

Figure 4.23: Committing and pushing to origin

We've seen how KDiff and similar programs can greatly reduce the amount of work involved in solving merge conflicts.

Merging from the command line

Much more common is for there to be a merge conflict when you specifically merge locally. To do so is pretty easy. From the command line, check out the branch you want to merge **into** (main) and then use the Git command merge:

```
> git co main
Switched to branch 'main'
Your branch is up to date with 'origin/main'.
SESA560987@DESKTOP-D21661F  C:\GitHub\VisualStudio\ProGitForProgrammers  main ≡
> git merge book
Merge made by the 'recursive' strategy.
 ProGitForProgrammers/ProGitForProgrammers/Book.cs | 14 ++++++++++++++
 1 file changed, 14 insertions(+)
 create mode 100644 ProGitForProgrammers/ProGitForProgrammers/Book.cs
```

Figure 4.24: The merge command

Here Git used the "recursive" strategy; a way to speed up the merge.

Fast forward

Often, however, you'll see Git report that it used a fast forward merge. Fast forward works like this; suppose your starting point is this:

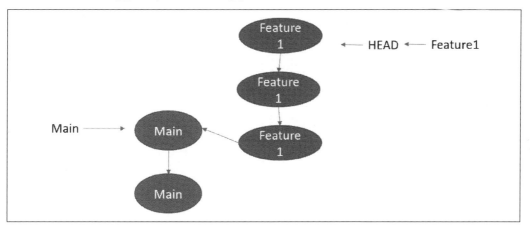

Figure 4.25: Fast forward

You now want to merge **Feature1** into **Main**. Notice that **Feature1** branched from the tip of **Main** (the latest commit). In that case, there is a path from the first commit in **Main** to the last commit in **Feature1**. In that case, all Git has to do is move **Main**'s pointer to the tip of **Feature1**, creating a single branch (which it will call **Main**):

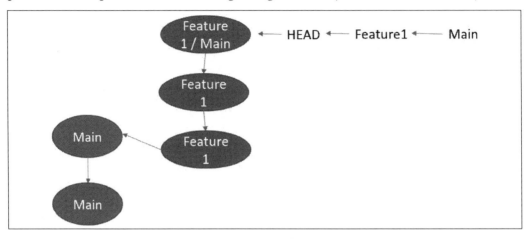

Figure 4.26: Moving the pointer

Because all that is required is moving a pointer to the last commit, this is called **fast forward**.

True merge

In the previous example, **Feature1** was branched off of **Main** at the point that is still the tip of **Main**. But what if someone else merged a branch into **Main**, and now the commit you branched off of is no longer the tip:

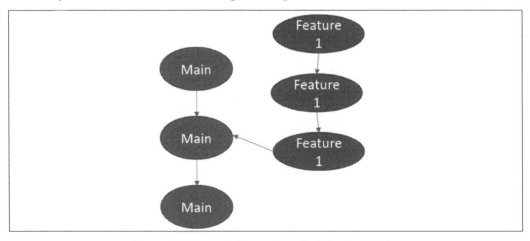

Figure 4.27: Feature 1 does not branch off the tip of Main

In this case, you either need a rebase (covered in the next chapter) or a "true" merge:

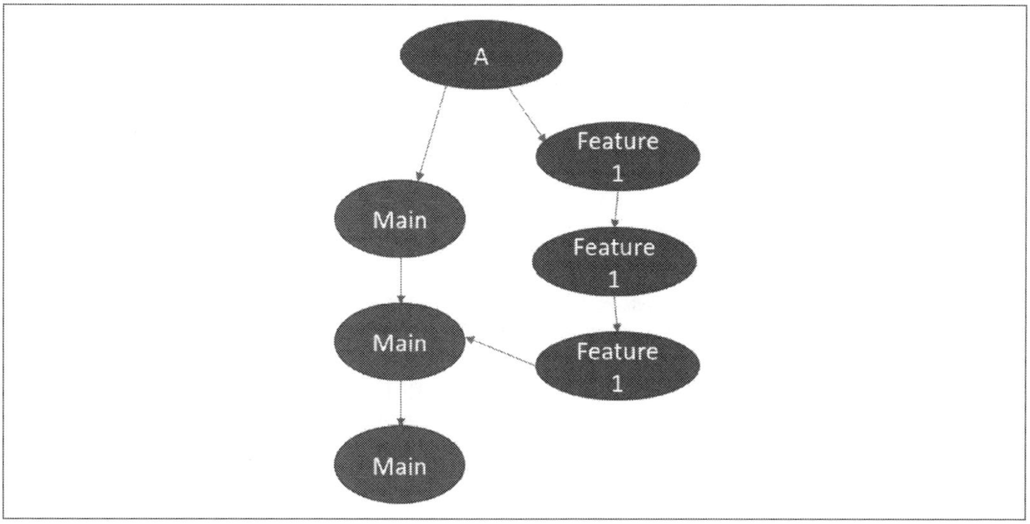

Figure 4.28: A true merge is required

Because there was no path from **Main** to the tip of **Feature1** that didn't leave out any other commits (for example, the tip of **Main**), we use a new commit to bring the two branches together.

Notice that this approach adds a new commit (**A**) that exists only for the merge. Over time you will have a lot of these relatively meaningless commits cluttering up your history. The solution to this is to rebase, as shown in the next chapter.

You don't change anything when doing a fast forward or a true merge; you merge and Git takes care of the details

Avoiding conflicts

Avoiding conflict is generally a good thing to do, and in the case of Git, it is a very good thing indeed. Rather than having to resolve a whole lot of conflicts all at once, you really want to catch those conflicts as you go (and thus handle just one or two at a time). If you are on a team, some conflicts cannot be avoided, but there are two good rules of thumb to cut down drastically on the work involved in handling conflicts:

- Do not have more than one programmer working on any given file (if possible)
- Merge main into your feature branch very frequently

Notice #2 does *not* say to merge your feature branch into main, but rather the other way around. This will not endanger the main thread, but will quickly reveal if there are any conflicts so far. If so, you can fix them in your branch and move on.

Summary

In this chapter, you saw:

- How to merge branches
- The different types of merges
- How to merge conflicts
- How tools like KDiff can make merging easier
- What a pull request is
- What a fast forward merge is
- What a true merge is

Challenge

Pretend you are two programmers working on the same project – a utility that contains a calculator and a Fahrenheit to Celsius converter. If you actually have two programmers to do this, even better.

Set up a new repository and clone it to two different folders. Have one person populate the main branch with the beginnings of the UtilityKnife project, commit the changes, and push it. Have the other person pull the main branch's changes.

OK, you both have a main branch with some code on it. Now have each programmer create their own branch, one to work on the calculator and the other to work on the converter. Along the way, the converter will want to use some of the methods of the calculator. Try to avoid or minimize conflicts, merge frequently, and resolve conflicts that arise.

Answer

As always, there is no one single correct way to do this. Here is how I worked through it.

Task #1: Set up a new repository and clone it to two different folders

Notice that we are going to use just one repository. We are building a single program, but at least at first John is going to create the calculator while Sara is going to create the temperature converter. We'll call the entire program **UtilityKnife**. To begin we go to GitHub.com and create our new repository:

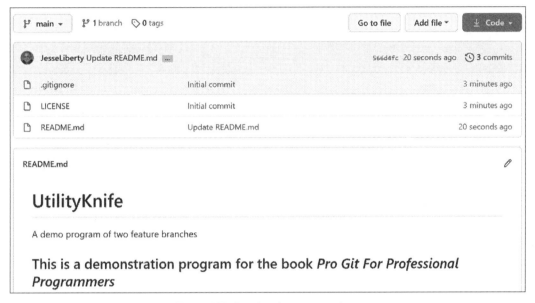

Figure 4.29: Creating the new repository

 The readme file is written using Markdown. You can learn more about Markdown at https://www.markdownguide.org/cheat-sheet/ among other places on the net.

We then clone the repo into folders (or separate computers if there are two or more of you). I'll create a directory, John, and clone this repo into that directory.

```
SESA560987@DESKTOP-D21661F ▶ C:\GitHub
> mkdir John


    Directory: C:\GitHub

Mode                 LastWriteTime         Length Name
----                 -------------         ------ ----
d----          2/15/2021  8:12 AM                 John

SESA560987@DESKTOP-D21661F ▶ C:\GitHub
> cd John
SESA560987@DESKTOP-D21661F ▶ C:\GitHub\John
> git clone git@github.com:JesseLiberty/UtilityKnife.git
Cloning into 'UtilityKnife'...
remote: Enumerating objects: 11, done.
remote: Counting objects: 100% (11/11), done.
remote: Compressing objects: 100% (11/11), done.
remote: Total 11 (delta 4), reused 0 (delta 0), pack-reused 0
Receiving objects: 100% (11/11), 5.20 KiB | 1.73 MiB/s, done.
Resolving deltas: 100% (4/4), done.
SESA560987@DESKTOP-D21661F ▶ C:\GitHub\John
> _
```

Figure 4.30: Cloning from the command line

John has chosen to use the command line. Sara, on the other hand, likes to use Visual Studio.

Begin by clicking on **File** and selecting **Clone Repository...**:

Figure 4.31: Opening the Git menu

That will bring up a dialog box where you can paste in the path you took from GitHub.com and the path to your new repo:

Figure 4.32: Cloning from Visual Studio

Click the **Clone** button, and Visual Studio will set up your cloned repository.

Solution Explorer validates that you have cloned the repository and brought down the three files from GitHub:

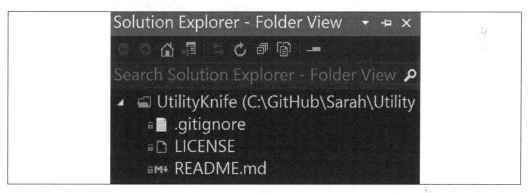

Figure 4.33: Solution Explorer shows results of the clone

Task #2: Have one person populate the main branch with the beginnings of UtilityKnife, commit the changes, and push it

We'll have Sara create a new solution in her directory for the UtilityKnife program:

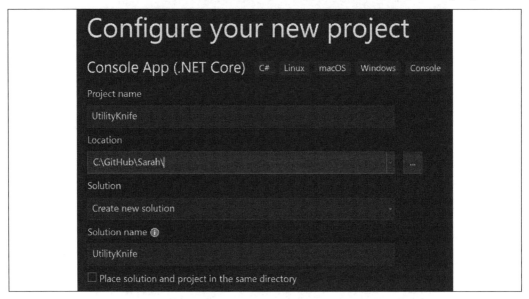

Figure 4.34: Creating the program

When the project is completed, she adjusts `Program.cs` to be the skeleton of all that is to come:

```
namespace UtilityKnife
{
    public static class Program
    {
        static void Main(string[] args)
        {
            // skeleton program
        }
    }
}
```

With this in place, she will commit these changes using the **Git** menu:

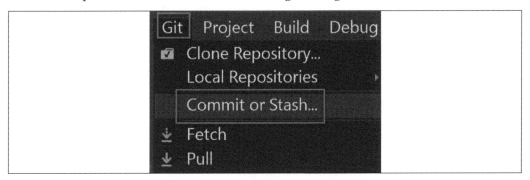

Figure 4.35: The Git menu in Visual Studio

This will open the commit window, where you can fill in the commit message, and then click **Commit All**:

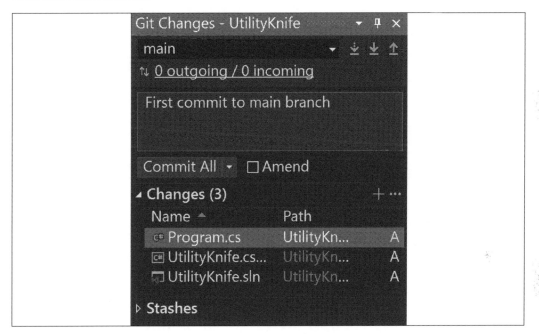

Figure 4.36: The Git Changes menu in Visual Studio

Once you do, the view will change to remove the files and commit message and will confirm the commit and show that there is one commit ready to be pushed:

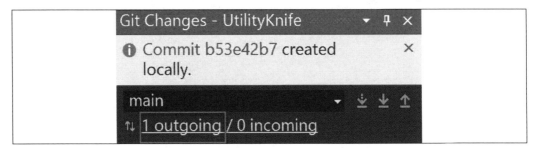

Figure 4.37: Commit confirmation in Visual Studio

That is just what we want, so click on the upload button (the up-pointing arrow) and push the commit to the repo on GitHub.

It verifies your success and offers to create a Pull Request for you, which we do not want right now:

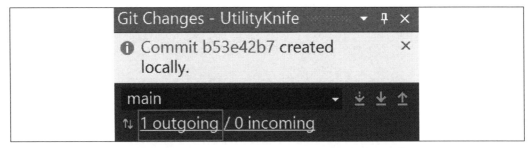

Figure 4.38: After commit Visual Studio indicates there is one file to push

Sara now has the starting main branch and is ready to create a feature branch. Before we look at that, let's have John bring down the main branch as well:

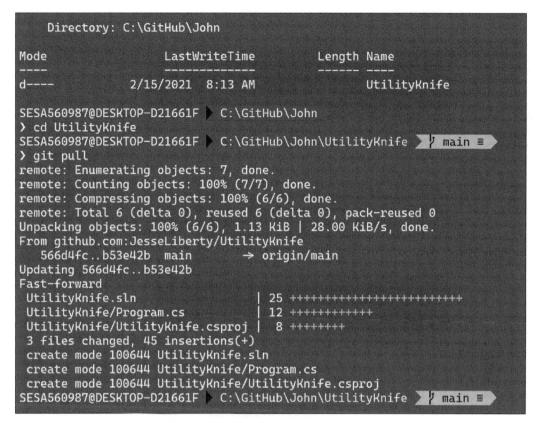

Figure 4.39: Pulling the repository from origin

This is a somewhat complex screenshot. We start by seeing that within `C:\GitHub\John` there is a folder called `UtilityKnife`. We change to that directory and then do a `git pull`. The result is the retrieval of the files for the `UtilityKnife` program.

Now both John and Sara have the same starter program for UtilityKnife.

Task #3: Each programmer creates a feature branch. Each programmer then puts the beginning of their feature into their branch, committing frequently (more frequently than you would in "real life")

John, who uses the command line, starts his feature branch by using the checkout -b command, which both creates a new branch and checks it out:

```
SESA560987@DESKTOP-D21661F  C:\GitHub\John\UtilityKnife   main ≡
> git checkout -b temperatureConverter
Switched to a new branch 'temperatureConverter'
SESA560987@DESKTOP-D21661F  C:\GitHub\John\UtilityKnife   temperatureConverter ≢
```

Figure 4.40: Creating a new branch at the command line

He is now ready to start coding. Let's create a folder, and then within that folder, the skeleton of our class and its first method:

```
namespace UtilityKnife.Converters
{
    public class FahrenheitToCelsius
    {
        public double FahrenheitToCelsiusConverter(double FahrenheitTemp)
        {
            double _fahreneithTemp = 0.0;
            double _celsius = 0.0;
            return _celsius;
        }
    }
}
```

Let's save and commit this:

```
> git status
On branch temperatureConverter
Untracked files:
  (use "git add <file>..." to include in what will be committed)


nothing added to commit but untracked files present (use "git add" to track)
SESA560987@DESKTOP-D21661F  C:\GitHub\John\UtilityKnife    temperatureConverter  +1 ~0 -0 !
> git add
SESA560987@DESKTOP-D21661F  C:\GitHub\John\UtilityKnife    temperatureConverter  +1 ~0 -0 ~
> git commit
[temperatureConverter 738a95f] Creaete skeleton for FtoC converter
 1 file changed, 10 insertions(+)
 create mode 100644 UtilityKnife/Converters/FahrenheitToCelsius.cs
SESA560987@DESKTOP-D21661F  C:\GitHub\John\UtilityKnife    temperatureConverter
```

Figure 4.41: Committing from the command line

We begin by taking a status that shows us that we have one untracked file. We add that file (remember that add . means add all the untracked and modified files to the index), and then we commit it, adding a message. Uh oh, the commit message is misspelled. Let's fix that with a new command: amend. Since we have not pushed, all we have to do is enter --amend and use -m for the revised message:

```
> git commit --amend -m "Create skeleton for FtoC converter"
[temperatureConverter 121012c] Create skeleton for FtoC converter
 Date: Mon Feb 15 15:29:40 2021 -0500
 1 file changed, 10 insertions(+)
 create mode 100644 UtilityKnife/Converters/FahrenheitToCelsius.cs
SESA560987@DESKTOP-D21661F  C:\GitHub\John\UtilityKnife    temperatureConverter
```

Figure 4.42: Using the amend flag

Notice the second line reflects back the change, and if we use log to see the commits, we'll see that the commit now is spelled correctly:

```
> git log --oneline
121012c (HEAD → temperatureConverter) Create skeleton for FtoC converter
```

Figure 4.43: Using log to see the commit

John decides to push his commit from his local repository up to the origin (the GitHub repo). When he tries, however, Git tells him that the server doesn't know about his branch, but it helpfully gives him the right command to use:

```
> git push
fatal: The current branch temperatureConverter has no upstream branch.
To push the current branch and set the remote as upstream, use

    git push --set-upstream origin temperatureConverter

SESA560987@DESKTOP-D21661F ▸ C:\GitHub\John\UtilityKnife ⟩ ⌥ temperatureConverter ≢
> git push --set-upstream origin temperatureConverter
Enumerating objects: 7, done.
Counting objects: 100% (7/7), done.
Delta compression using up to 16 threads
Compressing objects: 100% (5/5), done.
Writing objects: 100% (5/5), 584 bytes | 584.00 KiB/s, done.
Total 5 (delta 1), reused 0 (delta 0), pack-reused 0
remote: Resolving deltas: 100% (1/1), completed with 1 local object.
remote:
remote: Create a pull request for 'temperatureConverter' on GitHub by visiting:
remote:        https://github.com/JesseLiberty/UtilityKnife/pull/new/temperatureConverter
remote:
To github.com:JesseLiberty/UtilityKnife.git
 * [new branch]      temperatureConverter -> temperatureConverter
Branch 'temperatureConverter' set up to track remote branch 'temperatureConverter' from 'origin'.
SESA560987@DESKTOP-D21661F ▸ C:\GitHub\John\UtilityKnife ⟩ ⌥ temperatureConverter ≡
```

Figure 4.44: Trying to push but failing. Git helps.

Meanwhile, Sara has begun work on the Calculator class.

Sara and the Calculator

Within Visual Studio, she clicks on the **Git** menu choice and then **new branch**. A dialog opens, and note that it assumes you want to branch off of **main** (though if you have multiple branches, you can of course branch off of any of them):

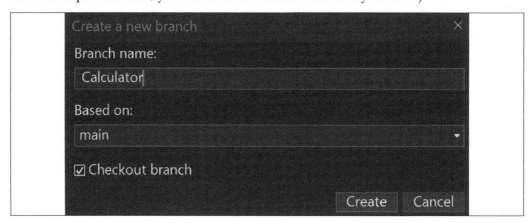

Figure 4.45: Creating a new branch

She is ready now to code, and whatever she writes will not affect John's code (or the code on main). You can verify that she can't even see John's work. They are on different (and thus isolated) feature branches.

She will add the skeleton of a `Calculator` class within its own folder.

```
namespace UtilityKnife.Calculator
{
    public class Calculator
    {
        public static int Add (int x, int y)
        {
            return x + y;
        }
    }
}
```

Sara will now check this in, but unlike John, she will not push it up to the server. Thus, it will be in her local repository only.

After selecting **Git | Commit** or **Stash**, she enters her message and clicks **Commit All**:

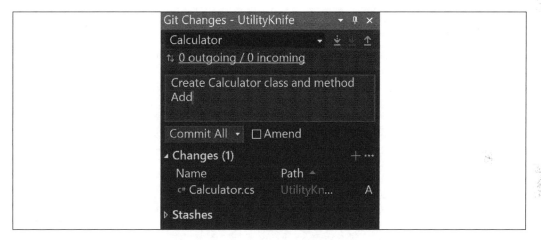

Figure 4.46: Committing all

As noted above, this puts her commit into the local repository.

Task #4: Merge the main branch into the feature branch frequently to ensure that if there are conflicts, you catch them early

John wants to merge main into his branch to ensure that he catches bugs early. To do this, he switches to main, updates by issuing a `pull` request, and then switches back to his feature branch and enters `merge main`:

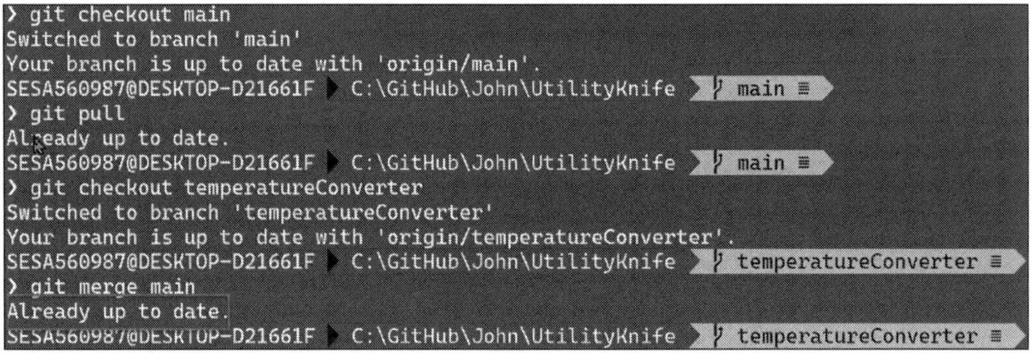

```
> git checkout main
Switched to branch 'main'
Your branch is up to date with 'origin/main'.
SESA560987@DESKTOP-D21661F  ▶  C:\GitHub\John\UtilityKnife  ⌥ main ≡
> git pull
Already up to date.
SESA560987@DESKTOP-D21661F  ▶  C:\GitHub\John\UtilityKnife  ⌥ main ≡
> git checkout temperatureConverter
Switched to branch 'temperatureConverter'
Your branch is up to date with 'origin/temperatureConverter'.
SESA560987@DESKTOP-D21661F  ▶  C:\GitHub\John\UtilityKnife  ⌥ temperatureConverter ≡
> git merge main
Already up to date.
SESA560987@DESKTOP-D21661F  ▶  C:\GitHub\John\UtilityKnife  ⌥ temperatureConverter ≡
```

Figure 4.47: Main already up to date

No problem here. Main hasn't changed since we branched off of it, so `temperatureConverter` is fully up to date.

Now, suppose John decides to merge his feature branch into main. Whether or not this is wise, all he has to do is reverse the merge order:

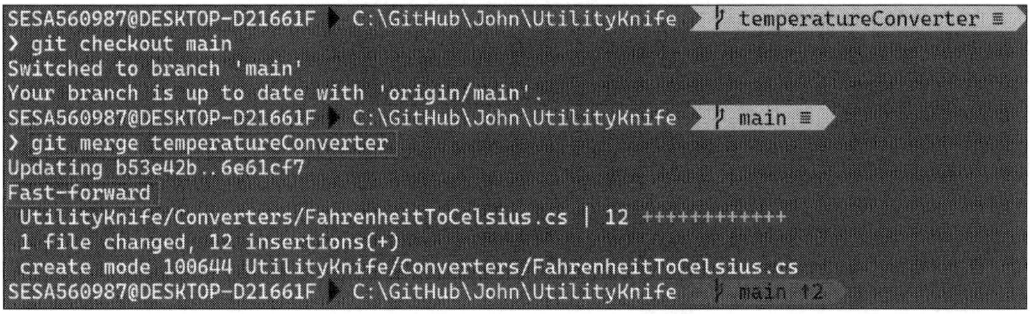

```
SESA560987@DESKTOP-D21661F  ▶  C:\GitHub\John\UtilityKnife  ⌥ temperatureConverter ≡
> git checkout main
Switched to branch 'main'
Your branch is up to date with 'origin/main'.
SESA560987@DESKTOP-D21661F  ▶  C:\GitHub\John\UtilityKnife  ⌥ main ≡
> git merge temperatureConverter
Updating b53e42b..6e61cf7
Fast-forward
 UtilityKnife/Converters/FahrenheitToCelsius.cs | 12 ++++++++++++
 1 file changed, 12 insertions(+)
 create mode 100644 UtilityKnife/Converters/FahrenheitToCelsius.cs
SESA560987@DESKTOP-D21661F  ▶  C:\GitHub\John\UtilityKnife  ⌥ main ↑2
```

Figure 4.48: Reversing the merge order

The key line here is:

```
git merge temperatureConverter
```

We are on the main branch, and this merges the feature branch into main. You can see that Git is able to fast-forward the merge, as described in a previous chapter.

John is now free to continue with his existing feature branch or to create a new one. If, on the other hand, he had to do a Pull Request and then wait for his PR to be approved before it is really merged, he would be wise to make a new branch, possibly off of `temperatureConverter`.

Sara had taken a break but she's ready to go back to work. Being cautious, she wants first to merge main into her feature branch to make sure there are no conflicts. Remember, John and Sara may work well together but they are not telling each other every time they commit or merge.

To start, Sara checks out main and does a `pull` to get the latest files from main. Now she checks out **Calculator** and right-clicks on **main**:

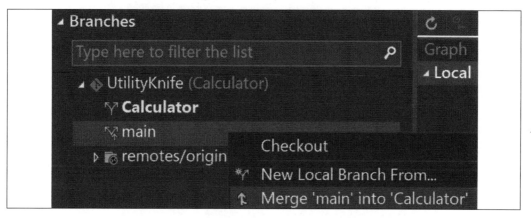

Figure 4.49: Merging main into Calculator in Visual Studio

She will select **Merge 'main' into 'Calculator'**. Once again, doing so will *not* merge her changes into main, but simply retrieve the newest version of main and merge that into her feature branch.

Since Visual Studio is cautious, it will ask you if you are sure.

Figure 4.50: Visual Studio checks that what you are about to do is what you want to do

Clicking **Yes** will begin the merge. Now, remember that John had done some work, and then merged his branch into main. Since there were no conflicts, Visual Studio just tells Sara that the merge was successful:

> ⓘ Repository updated to commit 6e61cf7d.

Figure 4.51: Visual Studio signals success

Of course, merging main into Calculator will change Calculator, bringing in everything in main. The key thing in main is what John merged, and we see that in Calculator now:

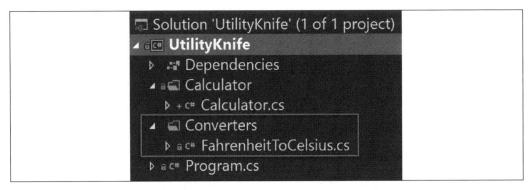

Figure 4.52: Examining the result of the merges in Visual Studio

Note that since Sara has not merged her code into main, John has no awareness of, nor way to get to, the Calculator class. If we open Visual Studio in John's branch, we see **Converters** but no **Calculator**:

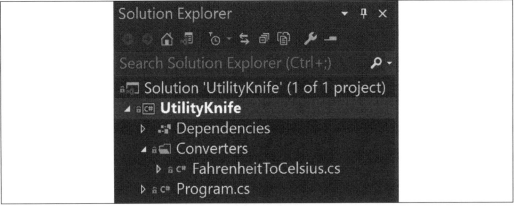

Figure 4.53: John's branch with no Calculator

Let's pause a moment and think about what is happening on GitHub. Sara has committed her changes but not pushed them, so GitHub won't know about her branch. John has pushed his changes and also merged them into main. We would anticipate two branches on GitHub, one for main and one for John; what's more, at this point, main and John should be identical, and Sara should have a branch on GitHub:

Figure 4.54: The branches on origin

Main has **Converters** (from John's merge) but not Calculator (because Sara has not merged). John's branch (**temperatureConverter**) is identical:

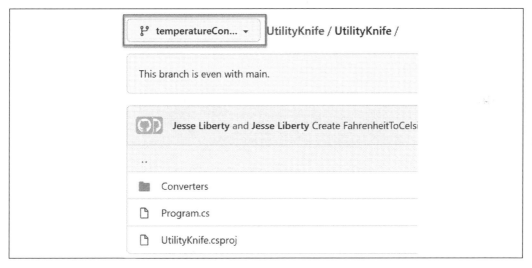

Figure 4.55: Changing branches on origin

To drive this home, we can ask GitHub for a list of all the branches it knows about:

Figure 4.56: Asking GitHub to list all the branches

 These all show as updated by me because Sara and John don't really exist.

Task #5: John is building the temperature converter. Have him "borrow" code from the calculator. See if there are merge conflicts

In the next four commits, Sara fleshes out the calculator with subtraction, multiplication, integer division, and division. She has not yet pushed her changes:

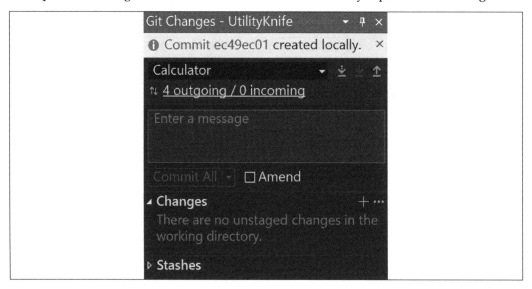

Figure 4.57: Fleshing out the calculator

The formula for converting Fahrenheit to Celsius is:

$$(F - 32) * 5/9$$

John wants to convert 212° Fahrenheit (the boiling point of water) and expects to get back 100° Celsius as a good test case. To do this, he could use the built-in subtraction and division operators but instead chooses to use Sara's calculator. His first attempt is to merge main into his branch:

```
> git checkout main
Switched to branch 'main'
Your branch is up to date with 'origin/main'.
SESA560987@DESKTOP-D21661F   C:\GitHub\John\UtilityKnife   ⎇ main ≡
> git pull
Already up to date.
SESA560987@DESKTOP-D21661F   C:\GitHub\John\UtilityKnife   ⎇ main ≡
> git checkout temperatureConverter
Switched to branch 'temperatureConverter'
Your branch is up to date with 'origin/temperatureConverter'.
SESA560987@DESKTOP-D21661F   C:\GitHub\John\UtilityKnife   ⎇ temperatureConverter ≡
> git merge main
Already up to date.
SESA560987@DESKTOP-D21661F   C:\GitHub\John\UtilityKnife   ⎇ temperatureConverter ≡
```

Figure 4.58: Merging main into the working branch

Main is up to date and there is no difference between main and temperatureConverter. Yet John doesn't have the functions he needs. This tells John that the calculator functions he needs are not yet pushed to GitHub. He can call Sara and ask her to push them so that he can pull them down, or she can merge them into main and then he can update from main. Sara is not ready to merge into main, but agrees to push her branch's commits.

She has four outgoing commits (that is, commits that have not yet been pushed to the origin):

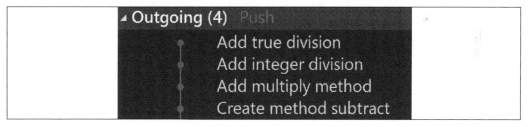

Figure 4.59: Visual Studio indicates four outgoing commits

To push these, she just clicks on the up arrow:

Figure 4.60: The push button in Visual Studio

John tries to bring down the changes but runs into a brick wall.

```
> git checkout Calculator
error: pathspec 'Calculator' did not match any file(s) known to git
SESA560987@DESKTOP-D21661F ▶ C:\GitHub\John\UtilityKnife ▶ temperatureConverter ☰
```

Figure 4.61: Unable to see Calculator

His local repository has never heard of the branch **Calculator**. There are a couple of ways to solve this but the easiest is to ask Sara to merge her work into **main**:

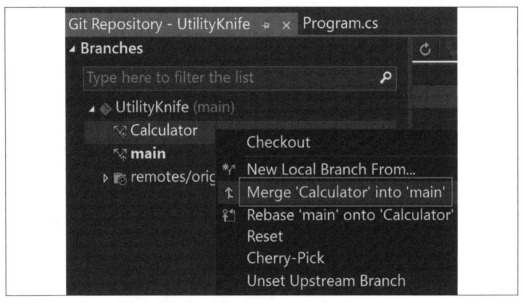

Figure 4.62: Merging Calculator into main

When Sara merges Calculator into main, she does so *locally*. She still has to push these changes to the origin to do John any good. She pushes as she would any commit.

John is now ready to `pull` these changes. Once he does, he realizes that Sara has used integers and he needs doubles. He modifies the `Calculator` class to use doubles, and while he is at it, he makes all the methods (and the class) static. (If you're not familiar with C#, don't worry about what that means; the important thing is that he's made a change)

```
namespace UtilityKnife.Calculator
{
    public static class Calculator
    {
        public static double Add(double x, double y)
        {
            return x + y;
        }
        public static double Subtract(double x, double y)
        {
            return x - y;
        }
        public static double Multiply(double x, double y)
        {
            return x * y;
        }

        public static int Division (int x, int y)
        {
            return x / y;
        }

        public static double Division (double x, double y)
        {
            return x / y;
        }

    }
}
```

```
> git checkout main
Switched to branch 'main'
Your branch is up to date with 'origin/main'.
SESA560987@DESKTOP-D21661F ▶ C:\GitHub\John\UtilityKnife ⑂ main ≡
> git pull
remote: Enumerating objects: 22, done.
remote: Counting objects: 100% (22/22), done.
remote: Compressing objects: 100% (5/5), done.
remote: Total 20 (delta 11), reused 20 (delta 11), pack-reused 0
Unpacking objects: 100% (20/20), 1.62 KiB | 12.00 KiB/s, done.
From github.com:JesseLiberty/UtilityKnife
   6e61cf7..ec49ec0  main        -> origin/main
 * [new branch]      Calculator  -> origin/Calculator
Updating 6e61cf7..ec49ec0
Fast-forward
 UtilityKnife/Calculator/Calculator.cs | 29 +++++++++++++++++++++++++++++
 1 file changed, 29 insertions(+)
 create mode 100644 UtilityKnife/Calculator/Calculator.cs
SESA560987@DESKTOP-D21661F ▶ C:\GitHub\John\UtilityKnife ⑂ main ≡
```

Figure 4.63: Pull the changes for the branch

The second line says that we're starting out with main up to date with origin/main. However, when we do a pull, the local Git finds objects to bring down for main. There are 22 objects. Why 22 when there were only 4 commits? Some of these objects are used internally by Git.

Later, we see that the merge was a fast forward, and the next line shows that there were 29 additions and no modifications or deletions (if you count the + marks, you'll find that there are 29). This is followed by the confirmation that 1 file changed with 29 insertions.

John is almost there. His local copy of main now has what he needs, but it is on the wrong branch. The solution is to merge main into temperatureConverter.

Because the order of which branch is being merged into the other matters, I always look it up on Stack Overflow:

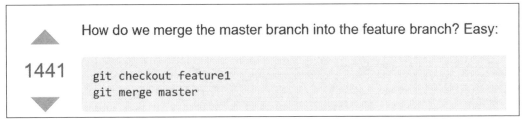

Figure 4.64: Stack Overflow advice

These are exactly the steps John needs to take:

```
> git checkout temperatureConverter
Switched to branch 'temperatureConverter'
Your branch is up to date with 'origin/temperatureConverter'.
SESA560987@DESKTOP-D21661F   C:\GitHub\John\UtilityKnife    temperatureConverter ≡
> git merge main
Updating 6e61c+7..ec49ec0
Fast-forward
 UtilityKnife/Calculator/Calculator.cs | 29 ++++++++++++++++++++++++++++++
 1 file changed, 29 insertions(+)
 create mode 100644 UtilityKnife/Calculator/Calculator.cs
SESA560987@DESKTOP-D21661F   C:\GitHub\John\UtilityKnife    temperatureConverter ↑4
```

Figure 4.65: Merging

The last two lines indicate that Calculator has been brought over with the merge and that temperatureConverter has two commits to push to its repo.

A quick look at the log shows that HEAD, origin/temperatureConverter, origin/main, origin/HEAD, and origin/Calculator are all pointing to the same commit as main! Thus, John's branch now has access to the Calculator class:

```
> git log --oneline
ec49ec0 (HEAD → temperatureConverter, origin/temperatureConverter, origin/main, origin/HEAD,
origin/Calculator, main) Add true division
```

Figure 4.66: Access to the calculator

He can now return to his program and use these static methods:

```
namespace UtilityKnife.Converters
{
    public class FahrenheitToCelsius
    {
        public double FahrenheitToCelsiusConverter(double fahrenheitTemp)
        {
            double _celsius = 0.0;

            // (F - 32) * 5/9

            var step1 = Calculator.Calculator.Subtract(
              fahrenheitTemp, 32);
            var step2 = Calculator.Calculator.Multiplication(
              step1, 5.0);
            _celsius = Calculator.Calculator.Division(step2, 9.0);
            return _celsius;
        }
    }
}
```

I agree that this is wicked ugly, but it works, and more importantly, it demonstrates that John's `temperatureConverter` can use code from `Calculator`. What's more, John can edit `Calculator`. We'll see what happens when all this is merged.

In jumping back and forth between John and Sara, I did the work in Sara's folder. No harm done, however. We'll just have Sara commit the changes. Uh oh, the changes were made on main. Let's clean all this up. First, on Sara's machine, let's merge main into `Calculator`:

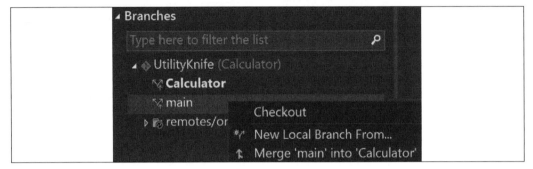

Figure 4.67: Merging main into Calculator in Visual Studio

This is just like the previous merges except that now `Calculator` is the checked-out branch and we right-click on main to get the **Merge 'main' into 'Calculator'** option. Now, to ensure that all is right with the world, merge Calculator back into main.

At this point, Sara's `main` and `Calculator` branches are identical, but John still doesn't have what he needs. Sara can now push main to the origin with a simple push.

John can now retrieve main, which should have the changes he needs:

```
> git checkout main
Switched to branch 'main'
Your branch is up to date with 'origin/main'.
SESA560987@DESKTOP-D21661F ▶ C:\GitHub\John\UtilityKnife   ⑂ main ≡
> git pull
remote: Enumerating objects: 13, done.
remote: Counting objects: 100% (13/13), done.
remote: Compressing objects: 100% (4/4), done.
remote: Total 7 (delta 2), reused 7 (delta 2), pack-reused 0
Unpacking objects: 100% (7/7), 865 bytes | 14.00 KiB/s, done.
From github.com:JesseLiberty/UtilityKnife
   ec49ec0..7cfd9b1  main       → origin/main
Updating ec49ec0..7cfd9b1
Fast-forward
 UtilityKnife/Calculator/Calculator.cs            | 12 ++++++------
 UtilityKnife/Converters/FahrenheitToCelsius.cs | 12 +++++++++---
 2 files changed, 15 insertions(+), 9 deletions(-)
SESA560987@DESKTOP-D21661F ▶ C:\GitHub\John\UtilityKnife   ⑂ main ≡
```

Figure 4.68: Retrieving main with changes

Great, main has what John needs, but he needs it on his branch. No problem, we'll merge main into `temperatureConverter`:

```
> git checkout temperatureConverter
Switched to branch 'temperatureConverter'
Your branch is up to date with 'origin/temperatureConverter'.
SESA560987@DESKTOP-D21661F ▶ C:\GitHub\John\UtilityKnife ⧉ temperatureConverter ☰ [08:27]
> git merge main
Updating ec49ec0..7cfd9b1
Fast-forward
 UtilityKnife/Calculator/Calculator.cs          | 12 ++++++
 UtilityKnife/Converters/FahrenheitToCelsius.cs | 12 +++++++++
 2 files changed, 15 insertions(+), 9 deletions(-)
SESA560987@DESKTOP-D21661F ▶ C:\GitHub\John\UtilityKnife ⧉ temperatureConverter ↑1[08:27]
```

Figure 4.69: Merging main into temperatureConverter

Let's go look at John's Fahrenheit converter and see if it is now up to date.

```
namespace UtilityKnife.Converters
{
    public class FahrenheitToCelsius
    {
        public double FahrenheitToCelsiusConverter(double fahrenheitTemp)
        {
            double _celsius = 0.0;

            // (F - 32) * 5/9

            var step1 = Calculator.Calculator.Subtract(
             fahrenheitTemp, 32);
            var step2 = Calculator.Calculator.Multiplication(
             step1, 5.0);
            _celsius = Calculator.Calculator.Division(step2, 9.0);
            return _celsius;
        }
    }
}
```

We can test that this worked by feeding the method 212 and hoping to get back 100. Let's turn to the program for that:

```
using System;
using UtilityKnife.Converters;

namespace UtilityKnife
{
```

```
public static class Program
{
    static void Main(string[] args)
    {
        var converter = new FahrenheitToCelsius();
        var celsius = converter.FahrenheitToCelsiusConverter(212.0);
        Console.WriteLine($"Fahrenheit temp of 212 is {celsius}.");
    }
}
}
```

Let's run our program:

Microsoft Visual Studio Debug Console

Fahrenheit temp of 212 is 100.

Figure 4.70: Testing the program

We have completed the challenge and managed all our branches. More important, the program works!

5
Rebasing, Amend, and Cherry-Picking

If you say "rebasing" to most novice Git programmers, they burst into tears and run screaming from the room. But the truth is that this is only because of how it is explained in so many books and magazines, where rebasing is (correctly but confusingly) shown with diagrams of commits being copied and moved along with dense and technical text.

In truth, rebasing is not hard to understand, and it is not hard to do if you understand what it is for. In this chapter, we will review rebasing without fear.

Rebasing is a command that allows you to take a feature branch and place it on the tip of another branch. We'll discuss how, and more importantly *why*, you would do this.

Amending is a quick command that allows you to modify the most recent commit. You can use this to add a file you forgot to put in the commit or to fix up a botched message.

Cherry-picking is the ability to take one or more commits from a branch and apply them onto the tip of another branch.

Git programmers describe these three commands as **rewriting history** and that is what they all have in common. Each has the ability to change how commits were added to the repository, and thus clean up your list of commits.

Rebasing

Rebasing is nothing more than taking one branch and adding it to the tip of another, where the tip is simply the last commit in the branch. For example, suppose you have the following structure:

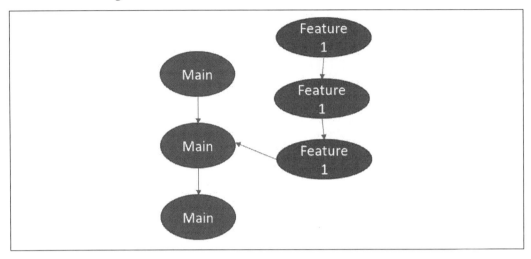

Figure 5.1: Git structure

You can't do a fast forward here, because **Main** has moved on since you branched from it. You can do a true merge, but a true merge adds a commit to your history every time you do one:

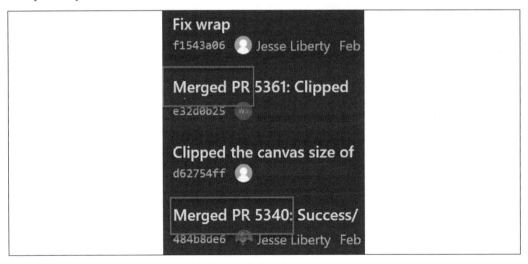

Figure 5.2: True merges

A rebase solves the same problem, but without adding merges to the commit history.

Notice that as you review this history, you have to skip over a significant number of commits since they are just merges. Rebase eliminates most of these commits.

Here comes the important part:

- You merge branch **Feature1** *into* **Main**, but you rebase **Feature1** *onto* **Main**.
- Returning to our earlier example, if you rebase **Feature1** onto **Main**, it looks like this:

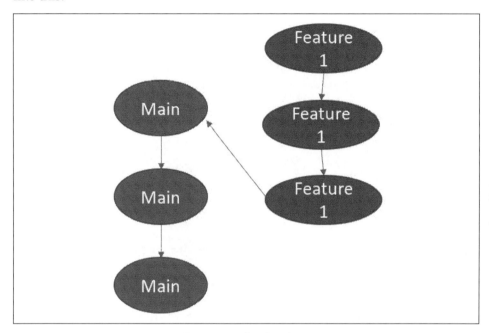

Figure 5.3: After the rebase

- There is now a clear path from the first commit of **Main** to the last commit of **Feature1** without leaving anything out. This is most often drawn like this:

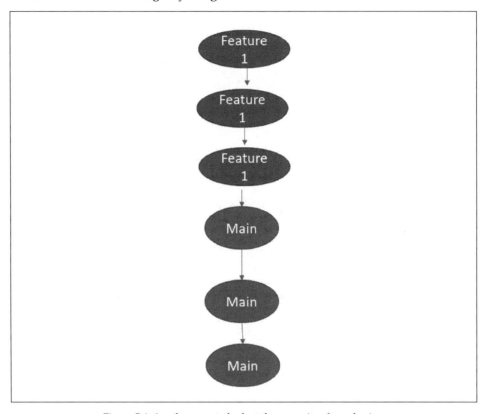

Figure 5.4: Another way to look at the commits after rebasing

- This emphasizes that you have rebased **Feature1** onto the tip of **Main** (the tip is **Main**'s latest commit).

That is all there is to rebasing. Honest.

How Git does it

Generally, I don't spend time or brain cells on how Git does what it does, but here it is worth noting that to rebase, Git rolls back history to the first **Feature1** commit and then makes a copy and adds it to the tip of **Main**. It then makes a copy of the second **Feature1** commit and puts that on top of the latest commit, and so forth.

The reason this is important is that a copy is made, and thus will have a different ID. Okay, you are now free to forget all this and treat rebasing as the magic it is.

Getting your head around it

Rebasing is not hard, as you have seen. But truly grokking what is happening and why it is okay takes anywhere from five minutes to five years. We are taking our feature and putting it on top of Main. Remember that our feature started as a branch off of Main.

Now we're incorporating all that is in Main into our feature.

That is the critical part. Because we do this locally, we are just saying "no matter how much Main has advanced, I will eventually need to merge into it. For now, I'm going to rebase onto Main, making it one long branch, and make sure there are no conflicts."

Rebase early and rebase often

It is very good practice to rebase frequently, so as to surface any conflicts that might arise. Each time you rebase, you end up with a stack of commits that has all that came before and then your new commits at the tip. If a conflict arises between what you just added and what was there, you will see it immediately and can fix it on the spot.

Rebase locally only

You rebase *only* on your local machine, and *never* on the shared repository in the cloud (for example, GitHub). This is because rebasing "rewrites history" – remember that it makes copies of Feature1 – and if another programmer is working on that branch, they will not be happy with you if you rebase. This is the kind of "not happy" that can lead to felony charges.

Rebasing in practice

Let's create a new repository named Rebasing. We're going to watch Adam as he creates a branch named Person by taking the following steps:

1. Go to the main root directory
2. Create a branch named Person
3. Open Visual Studio and create a project named Person
4. Create a new class named Person
5. Add the Rebasing repo to your local repository
6. Add the repository and commit it (which will also commit Person)

7. Add an age property to `Person` and commit (but don't push):

```
namespace Rebasing
{
    public class Person
    {
        public double Age {get; set;}
    }
}
```

8. Add a name property and commit but don't push

After we add a height property, we are in this situation:

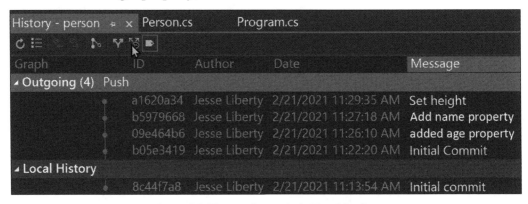

Figure 5.5: History of commits in Visual Studio

We could push now, but there is more work to be done on the `Person` class. On the other hand, we don't want main to have moved so far away from us that we'll have too many conflicts when we are done with person. The answer: rebase. Make sure you are on person, then right-click on main and choose **Rebase 'person' onto 'main'**:

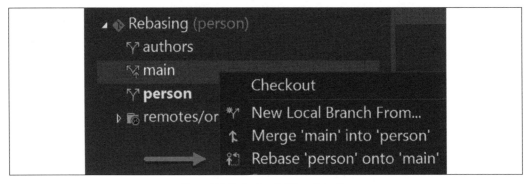

Figure 5.6: Rebasing in Visual Studio

With that done, we can continue working on the `Person` branch.

Notice that you have only four outgoing commits:

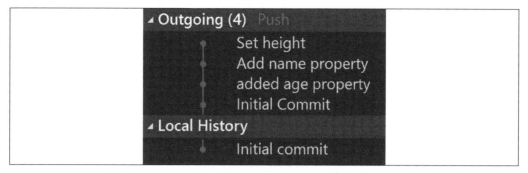

Figure 5.7: Rebasing does not add a commit

The rebase did not add a commit, and keeps your history clean.

Seeing the rebase at work

To see that your rebase did actually rewind the history of your commits and then add each commit back on top of main, go to the command line and issue the command `git log --name-only --oneline`:

```
SESA560987@DESKTOP-D21661F ▶ C:\GitHub\Rebasing ⟫ ⌥ person ≢
> git log --name-only --oneline
d61ffe0 (HEAD → person) Set height
Rebasing/Rebasing/Person.cs
6da241a Add name property
Rebasing/Rebasing/Person.cs
75c3382 added age property
Rebasing/Rebasing/Person.cs
7d77c7b Initial Commit
Rebasing/Rebasing.sln
Rebasing/Rebasing/Person.cs
Rebasing/Rebasing/Program.cs
Rebasing/Rebasing/Rebasing.csproj
8c44f7a (origin/main, origin/HEAD, main, authors) Initial commit
.gitignore
LICENSE
README.md
SESA560987@DESKTOP-D21661F ▶ C:\GitHub\Rebasing ⟫ ⌥ person ≢
```

Figure 5.8: Rebase rewinds history

What we see here going from top to bottom is the addition of the final property (height) and then we rebase `Person.cs` and add the name property. Next, we rebase and add the age property. We continue this all the way back until we've rebased all of the files onto the tip of main.

Conflicts

When rebasing we may well run into conflicts. You will remember that we have one branch: `Person`. Let's have a second programmer clone the repository. That second programmer is happily working away in their branch (teacher) when they realize they need person to have a different age. They add this to the file (okay, no one is quite that stupid, but this kind of thing happens in more subtle ways):

```
> git rebase main
error: could not apply cb76bd6 ... set age to 30
Resolve all conflicts manually, mark them as resolved with
"git add/rm <conflicted_files>", then run "git rebase --continue".
You can instead skip this commit: run "git rebase --skip".
To abort and get back to the state before "git rebase", run "git rebase --abort".
Could not apply cb76bd6 ... set age to 30
Auto-merging Rebasing/Rebasing/Person.cs
CONFLICT (content): Merge conflict in Rebasing/Rebasing/Person.cs
```

Figure 5.9: Rebasing caused conflicts

Fortunately, Git tells you what to do.

Remember, you can at any time enter `git rebase --abort` and go back to where you were before you started the rebase.

This time, however, we'll fix the problem by hand. Open the file pointed to Person.cs:

```
namespace Rebasing
{
    public class Person
    {

<<<<<<< HEAD
        public double Age { get; set; } = 35;
=======
        public double Age { get; set; } = 30;
>>>>>>> cb76bd6 (set age to 30)
        public string Name { get; set; }
```

```
        public double Height { get; set; }
        public double Weight { get; set; }

<<<<<<< HEAD
=======

>>>>>>> cb76bd6 (set age to 30)
    }
}
```

The part that looks like this:

```
<<<<<<< HEAD
        public double Age { get; set; } = 35;
=======
```

is the code in the current revision; the next set of code:

```
>>>>>>> cb76bd6 (set age to 30)
        public string Name { get; set; }
        public double Height { get; set; }
        public double Weight { get; set; }

<<<<<<< HEAD
```

is coming from the code to be rebased.

Bleh. What a mess. You can fix this by hand, making the adjustments and then removing the conflict markers, or you can use a tool as mentioned in the previous chapter.

To fix this, we'll adjust the age in the branch onto which we rebase the patches; i.e. 35 is the authoritative age, therefore the 35 line is the one we want to keep, and we want to remove the rest.

In any case, once you have resolved the conflicts, return to the command line and enter git rebase --continue. This will resume the rebase, checking for other conflicts. If there are none, Git will ask you to enter a message and the rebase will be completed:

```
> git rebase --continue
[detached HEAD 5843a73] Rebased, set age to 30
 1 file changed, 1 insertion(+)
Successfully rebased and updated refs/heads/person.
```

The key with rebase conflicts is not to panic, but to work your way through them one by one. Take heart, had you not done the rebase, you would have run into these issues and more when trying to merge into main once you were done with your feature branch.

Amending

If you check in a change and then realize you've left out a file or have mangled the message, you can use the amend command. However, you can only amend the most recent commit.

Let's say we return to person and we add a weight property and then commit it. Before we push it, we realize we left out a change to `Program.cs`:

```
namespace Rebasing
{
    class Program
    {
        static void Main(string[] args)
        {
            var person = new Person();
            person.Name = "Jesse";
        }
    }
}
```

Since the error was in the most recent commit, we can amend that commit. All we need to do is put the `Program.cs` file into the index and then issue the command `git commit --amend`.

Because amend rewrites history, **you must do this only before you push** (that is, while the commit is only in your local repo), for the same reasons as noted above:

```
SESA560987@DESKTOP-D21661F   C:\GitHub\Rebasing   person ↑1
> git add rebasing/rebasing/program.cs
SESA560987@DESKTOP-D21661F   C:\GitHub\Rebasing   person ↑1
> git commit --amend
[person f5eba62] add person and in person add weight
 Date: Sun Feb 21 11:48:14 2021 -0500
 1 file changed, 5 insertions(+), 3 deletions(-)
SESA560987@DESKTOP-D21661F   C:\GitHub\Rebasing   person ↑1
> _
```

Figure 5.10: Amending (before pushing!)

Let's take this one line at a time from the top. First we notice that one commit is waiting to be pushed. That is the commit we're going to amend.

On the second line, we add the file we want to amend to the index.

Next, we add the amend command: `git commit --amend`.

Git will respond by opening your editor so that you can amend the message (which we see here: `add person and in person add weight`).

Finally, it tells you all the usual information about the commit.

Notice, however, that you still have only one commit waiting to be pushed. The amend did not appear to create a new commit (okay, technically it did, but you can safely ignore that).

If you use a commit with no file name but with the message flag, you change only the message for that most recent commit. You don't even need the flag; if there are no new, modified, or deleted files in the index, it will open your editor for you:

```
SESA560987@DESKTOP-D21661F ▶ C:\GitHub\Rebasing    person ↑1
> git add rebasing/rebasing/program.cs
SESA560987@DESKTOP-D21661F ▶ C:\GitHub\Rebasing    person ↑1
> git commit --amend
[person f5eba62] add person and in person add weight
 Date: Sun Feb 21 11:48:14 2021 -0500
 1 file changed, 5 insertions(+), 3 deletions(-)
SESA560987@DESKTOP-D21661F ▶ C:\GitHub\Rebasing    person ↑1
>
```

Figure 5.11: This will cause your editor to open

If you get the history now, with log, you'll see the amended message:

```
> git log --oneline
3174c3b (HEAD → person) Add person and Person's weight property
d61ffe0 (origin/person) Set height
6da241a Add name property
75c3382 added age property
7d77c7b Initial Commit
8c44f7a (origin/main, origin/HEAD, main, authors) Initial commit
```

Figure 5.12: The message amended in the editor

Amend can save you a lot of work down the road, and it is important to have a well-written message to clarify the purpose of the commit.

Cherry-picking

Sometimes you just need one or a small number of commits from one branch to be added to the tip of another branch. A common case is this: you have a release branch and a feature branch. The release branch is "frozen" but then you need to add a commit from a feature branch to the release branch (possibly a patch to fix a problem). When you cherry-pick, the picked commit goes to the tip of the branch you are cherry-picking onto.

An illustration will help. Here's our starting point:

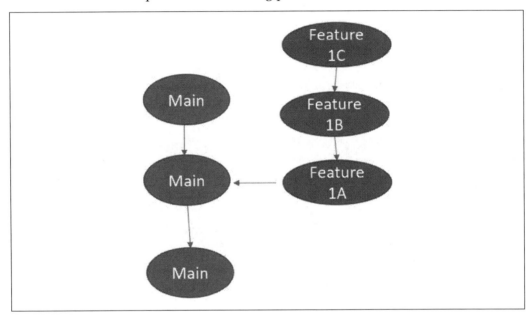

Figure 5.13: Before cherry-picking

We discover that we do not want all of **Feature1** on **Main**, but we do want **Feature1B** (it has the fix or feature set we need). To do this at the command line you enter git cherry-pick a2cb5f3 where a2cb5f3 is the ID of the feature commit you want to cherry-pick.

What you end up with looks like this:

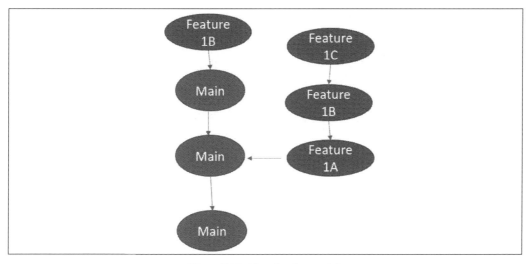

Figure 5.14: After the cherry-pick

Notice that **Feature1B** is now added to the tip of main, but it is also left on the feature branch.

Visual Studio cherry-picking

Visual Studio has terrific support for cherry-picking. Just go to the branch you want and then open the history. Right-click on the commit you want and choose **Cherry-Pick**:

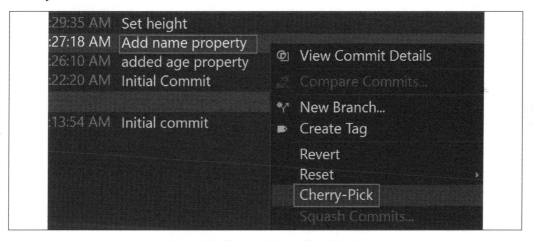

Figure 5.15: Cherry-picking in Visual Studio

Cherry-picking can be essential when you've branched off your develop branch but create something on a feature branch that you realize you need.

Summary

In this chapter, we looked at a few advanced topics:

- Rebasing
- Amending
- Cherry-picking

What all three of these have in common is that they all rewrite history. Rebasing does so by copying all the commits of one branch onto the tip of another. Amending does so by allowing you to add files and/or change the message on a commit. Finally, cherry-picking acts like rebasing, but using just one or a few commits.

You saw that many of these activities are easier in Visual Studio but that some things you want to do are much clearer at the command line.

Finally, we explained why you merge *into* main, but you rebase *onto* main.

Challenge

Create a new repository called Panofy, which supplies MP3 music to its subscribers. There will be three branches: main, which you get when you create the repo, and two feature branches. Demonstrate the following:

- Creating the repository
- Two programmers creating feature branches
- Frequent rebasing
- Amending a commit to add a file
- Amending a commit to change the message
- Cherry-picking one commit onto main

Answer

Once again, there are many ways to solve this challenge. Here is how I went about it.

Creating a new repository on GitHub

We've seen this before, so I'll do it quickly. I'll navigate to GitHub.com and fill in the usual form, making this demo program public:

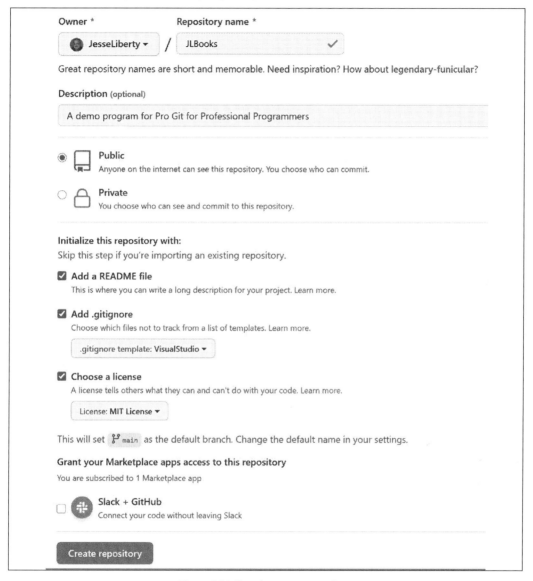

Figure 5.16: Creating a new repository

Once you've created the repository, you and anyone else who wants to develop against it (and has the right permissions) can clone it locally.

Creating two feature branches with fake programmers

To do this, I'll create two directories, and clone to each. My first directory I'll call GitHub/DirA and my second GitHub/DirB. I will then clone into each:

```
> cd DirA
SESA560987@DESKTOP-D21661F ▶ C:\GitHub\DirA
> git clone git@github.com:JesseLiberty/Panofy.git
Cloning into 'Panofy'...
remote: Enumerating objects: 5, done.
remote: Counting objects: 100% (5/5), done.
remote: Compressing objects: 100% (5/5), done.
remote: Total 5 (delta 0), reused 0 (delta 0), pack-reused 0
Receiving objects: 100% (5/5), done.
SESA560987@DESKTOP-D21661F ▶ C:\GitHub\DirA
```

Figure 5.17: Cloning the program to the local repository

Only Mateo will program in DirA, and only Kim will program in DirB.

Create a C# program in both DirA and DirB. Once done, use git status to ensure they are both pointing to main. To be certain, make a small change in DirA and make sure it is reflected in DirB. It is easy to become confused as to which directory your Visual Studio is pointing to. You can always right-click on the project and choose **Open folder in File Explorer** to double-check.

The steps I'll take to confirm that both directories have the same main branch are:

1. In branch B I will make a change and push it
2. In branch A I will pull the change to make my local repository
3. Finally, I will inspect Visual Studio in branch A to prove that it is identical to branch B:

```
[main c507abf] Add Hello message
 1 file changed, 1 insertion(+)
SESA560987@DESKTOP-D21661F ▶ C:\GitHub\DirB\Panofy    ⑂ main ↑1
> git push
Enumerating objects: 9, done.
Counting objects: 100% (9/9), done.
Delta compression using up to 16 threads
Compressing objects: 100% (5/5), done.
Writing objects: 100% (5/5), 513 bytes | 256.00 KiB/s, done.
Total 5 (delta 3), reused 0 (delta 0), pack-reused 0
remote: Resolving deltas: 100% (3/3), completed with 3 local objects.
To github.com:JesseLiberty/Panofy.git
   3c9929c..c507abf  main -> main
SESA560987@DESKTOP-D21661F ▶ C:\GitHub\DirB\Panofy    ⑂ main ≡
> cd ../../DirA/Panofy
SESA560987@DESKTOP-D21661F ▶ C:\GitHub\DirA\Panofy    ⑂ main ≡
> git pull
remote: Enumerating objects: 9, done.
remote: Counting objects: 100% (9/9), done.
remote: Compressing objects: 100% (2/2), done.
remote: Total 5 (delta 3), reused 5 (delta 3), pack-reused 0
Unpacking objects: 100% (5/5), 493 bytes | 13.00 KiB/s, done.
From github.com:JesseLiberty/Panofy
   3c9929c..c507abf  main        -> origin/main
Updating 3c9929c..c507abf
Fast-forward
 Panofy/Panofy/Program.cs | 1 +
 1 file changed, 1 insertion(+)
SESA560987@DESKTOP-D21661F ▶ C:\GitHub\DirA\Panofy    ⑂ main ≡
> _
```

Figure 5.18: Cloning to ensure the two repositories are identical

To keep track of what I'm looking at, I changed the name of the project for B to PanofyB. I then pushed that and on A I pulled it, so that both stay in sync.

This approach is fraught with danger, not least of which is that it is easy to overwrite the work of another developer, or to create conflicts. To avoid that, I'll create a branch for each programmer. I'll create a branch called Calculator on A and a branch called Converter on B.

Frequent rebasing

Now that we have two branches, and to keep this simple, we'll build a new version of UtilityKnife, this time with small features and frequent merging. Mateo will go first, creating the structure of the calculator, checking it in and you would merge it into main (you would not normally do it this way – you would build a few aspects of the feature, checking it in frequently, and then when you are done merging it, but we need some demo code).

When I first add to `Calculator`, main is identical, so when I rebase, essentially nothing happens:

```
SESA560987@DESKTOP-D21661F   C:\GitHub\DirA\Panofy     calculator ≢
> git status
On branch calculator
nothing to commit, working tree clean
SESA560987@DESKTOP-D21661F   C:\GitHub\DirA\Panofy     calculator ≢
> git checkout main
Switched to branch 'main'
Your branch is up to date with 'origin/main'.
SESA560987@DESKTOP-D21661F   C:\GitHub\DirA\Panofy     main ≡
> git pull
Already up to date.
SESA560987@DESKTOP-D21661F   C:\GitHub\DirA\Panofy     main ≡
> git checkout calculator
Switched to branch 'calculator'
SESA560987@DESKTOP-D21661F   C:\GitHub\DirA\Panofy     calculator ≢
> git rebase main
Current branch calculator is up to date.
SESA560987@DESKTOP-D21661F   C:\GitHub\DirA\Panofy     calculator ≢
```

Figure 5.19: Rebase early and Rebase often

Let's do a bit of work on `Calculator` and then get ready to push it. Before we do, however, let's do a rebase, in case work was done and pushed to main on a different thread:

```
> git checkout main
Switched to branch 'main'
Your branch is up to date with 'origin/main'.
SESA560987@DESKTOP-D21661F ▶ C:\GitHub\DirA\Panofy ⑂ main ≡
> git pull
remote: Enumerating objects: 8, done.
remote: Counting objects: 100% (8/8), done.
remote: Compressing objects: 100% (2/2), done.
remote: Total 5 (delta 3), reused 5 (delta 3), pack-reused 0
Unpacking objects: 100% (5/5), 541 bytes | 14.00 KiB/s, done.
From github.com:JesseLiberty/Panofy
    2ca4ad9..8d47c04  main          → origin/main
Updating 2ca4ad9..8d47c04
Fast-forward
 Panofy/Panofy/Converter.cs | 15 +++++++++++++++
 1 file changed, 15 insertions(+)
 create mode 100644 Panofy/Panofy/Converter.cs
SESA560987@DESKTOP-D21661F ▶ C:\GitHub\DirA\Panofy ⑂ main ≡
> git checkout calculator
Switched to branch 'calculator'
SESA560987@DESKTOP-D21661F ▶ C:\GitHub\DirA\Panofy ⑂ calculator ≢
> git rebase main
Successfully rebased and updated refs/heads/calculator.
SESA560987@DESKTOP-D21661F ▶ C:\GitHub\DirA\Panofy ⑂ calculator ≢
```

Figure 5.20: Pull changes and then get calculator, remembering to rebase onto main

Yes! Even though another thread (in this case converter) is added to main, we were able to rebase calculator's code on top of it. We now know that there will be no conflicts, at least so far in development.

Amending a commit to add a file

Let's return to the Calculator class. We'll add a division example using doubles, check it in, and commit it:

```
> git status
On branch calculator
Changes not staged for commit:
  (use "git add <file>..." to update what will be committed)
  (use "git restore <file>..." to discard changes in working directory)


no changes added to commit (use "git add" and/or "git commit -a")
SESA560987@DESKTOP-D21661F ▶ C:\GitHub\DirA\Panofy ⑂ calculator ≢ +0 ~1 -0 !
> git commit -a -m "Add divide using doubles"
[calculator 26b5ba0] Add divide using doubles
 1 file changed, 5 insertions(+)
SESA560987@DESKTOP-D21661F ▶ C:\GitHub\DirA\Panofy ⑂ calculator ≢
```

Figure 5.21: Using amend to add a file to the most recent commit

After we make the commit, we realize that we intended to add a square root method as well:

```
public double SquareRoot(double x)
{
    return Math.Sqrt(x);
}
```

We'd rather not create a new commit just for that. What we want to do is amend the most recent commit. We do that with the --amend command.

To do this, we put the file(s) we want to add into the index and issue the `git commit --amend` command:

```
> git status
On branch calculator
Changes not staged for commit:
  (use "git add <file>..." to update what will be committed)
  (use "git restore <file>..." to discard changes in working directory)
        modified:   Panofy/Panofy/Calculator.cs

no changes added to commit (use "git add" and/or "git commit -a")
SESA560987@DESKTOP-D21661F ▶ C:\GitHub\DirA\Panofy  calculator ≢ +0 ~1 -0 !
> git add .
SESA560987@DESKTOP-D21661F ▶ C:\GitHub\DirA\Panofy  calculator ≢ +0 ~1 -0 ~
> git commit --amend
[calculator 6fa0c30] Add divide using doubles and square root function
 Date: Mon Feb 22 14:00:28 2021 -0500
 1 file changed, 10 insertions(+)
SESA560987@DESKTOP-D21661F ▶ C:\GitHub\DirA\Panofy  calculator ≢
```

Figure 5.22: Amending the commit to include the change in Calculator.cs

We take the following steps in the code shown above:

1. Call git status. Note that we have a modified file, so add it to the index with git add.

2. Invoke git commit --amend, which commits the new code as part of the previous commit.

3. The editor will open; put in the new message. Notice that the new message is now displayed (second arrow).

This allows us to amend the message to something more meaningful. You'll see another way to do this in the chapter on interactive rebasing.

Amending a commit to change the message

If there is nothing new in the index then git commit --amend will just give you an opportunity to change the message:

```
> git status
On branch calculator
nothing to commit, working tree clean
SESA560987@DESKTOP-D21661F ▶ C:\GitHub\DirA\Panofy     calculator ≢
> git commit --amend -m "Add real divide and square root"
[calculator e49fd3d] Add real divide and square root
 Date: Mon Feb 22 14:00:28 2021 -0500
 1 file changed, 10 insertions(+)
SESA560987@DESKTOP-D21661F ▶ C:\GitHub\DirA\Panofy     calculator ≢
>
```

Figure 5.23: Using amend to modify the message of the most recent commit

We do a git status to make sure that nothing is in the index. We then call git commit --amend just as we did before, but we add a message (if we didn't add a message our editor would come up). Since there was nothing in the index, Git just changes the messages.

Cherry-picking one commit onto main

Here is the log for main and for calculator:

```
> git log --oneline main
8d47c04 (origin/main, origin/HEAD, main) add converter skeleton
2ca4ad9 add subtract method
877348c Update csproj
c507abf Add Hello message
3c9929c Sync'ing with B
2661adc fix conflicts
edd7b01 Initial files from DirA
da77c91 First use of Panofy in Dir B
a253788 Initial commit
SESA560987@DESKTOP-D21661F ▶ C:\GitHub\DirA\Panofy     calculator ≢
> git log --oneline calculator
e49fd3d (HEAD → calculator) Add real divide and square root
972d77a add multiply and divide
8d47c04 (origin/main, origin/HEAD, main) add converter skeleton
2ca4ad9 add subtract method
877348c Update csproj
c507abf Add Hello message
3c9929c Sync'ing with B
2661adc fix conflicts
edd7b01 Initial files from DirA
da77c91 First use of Panofy in Dir B
a253788 Initial commit
SESA560987@DESKTOP-D21661F ▶ C:\GitHub\DirA\Panofy     calculator ≢
```

Figure 5.24: Cheryy-pick onto main

We don't want to merge all of calculator into main but we do want to add the multiply and divide commits.

 Okay, that is silly, but for a real-world example imagine that main is your release branch, and calculator has an important function that you want to add.

Notice the seven-integer ID next to each commit. To cherry-pick 972d77a into main, we make sure main is the current branch and then we issue the cherry-pick command with the ID of the commit we want to add:

```
> git checkout main
Switched to branch 'main'
Your branch is up to date with 'origin/main'.
SESA560987@DESKTOP-D21661F ▶ C:\GitHub\DirA\Panofy ⑂ main ≡
> git cherry-pick 972d77a
[main 84bc465] add multiply and divide
 Date: Mon Feb 22 12:57:14 2021 -0500
 1 file changed, 11 insertions(+)
SESA560987@DESKTOP-D21661F ▶ C:\GitHub\DirA\Panofy ⑂ main ↑1
```

Figure 5.25: Issuing the cherry-pick command

You have committed 972d77a into main, and main has one commit to push. Before we push let's look at those logs again:

```
> git log --oneline main
84bc465 (HEAD -> main) add multiply and divide  ←————
8d47c04 (origin/main, origin/HEAD) add converter skeleton
2ca4ad9 add subtract method
877348c Update csproj
c507abf Add Hello message
3c9929c Sync'ing with B
2661adc fix conflicts
edd7b01 Initial files from DirA
da77c91 First use of Panofy in Dir B
a253788 Initial commit
SESA560987@DESKTOP-D21661F ▶ C:\GitHub\DirA\Panofy    ⑂ main ↑1
> git log --oneline calculator
e49fd3d (calculator) Add real divide and square root
972d77a add multiply and divide  ←————
8d47c04 (origin/main, origin/HEAD) add converter skeleton
2ca4ad9 add subtract method
877348c Update csproj
c507abf Add Hello message
3c9929c Sync'ing with B
2661adc fix conflicts
edd7b01 Initial files from DirA
da77c91 First use of Panofy in Dir B
a253788 Initial commit
```

Figure 5.26: Examining the log after the cherry-pick

Three things to notice here:

1. Main now has the add multiply and divide commit
2. Multiply and divide have not been removed from calculator
3. The ID is different for the two commits, meaning they are separate commits and manipulation of one will not affect the other

This example answer meets the requirements of creating two feature branches off a new repo, and the "programmers" rebase frequently. We also amended a message (while local) and used cherry-picking to copy one commit onto the main branch.

6

Interactive Rebasing

Interactive rebasing is a confusing name for a very useful Git functionality. From a user's perspective, rebase and interactive rebase have little in common.

Interactive rebase allows you to clean up your commits, but only *before* you push them to the server. With interactive rebasing you can:

- "Squash" your commits so that your commit history is sparser and easier to read
- Modify the message for your commits
- Fixup, which is just like squash except that it doesn't stop and ask for a new message
- Drop, which removes a commit

The key thing here is that you are modifying commits, not the files that go into a commit. And, as I'll keep mentioning, you must do this interactive rebasing *before* you push your commits to origin. You never modify commits once they are on the server because other developers may be interacting with the commits, and you will likely create conflicts, which are time-consuming to repair. See *Chapter 4, Merging, Pull Requests and Handling Merge Conflicts*, for information on merge conflicts.

Interactive rebasing at work

To see this at work, we need a dozen commits. Let's create a new quick and dirty program and create commits with every line. Once we have that, we can look at how interactive rebasing is accomplished at the command line and also in Visual Studio.

Note: you would never commit this frequently, but we need commits to work with.

Creating our example

For variety's sake, let's create the skeleton of a music tracking application. The first step is to create the repository on GitHub:

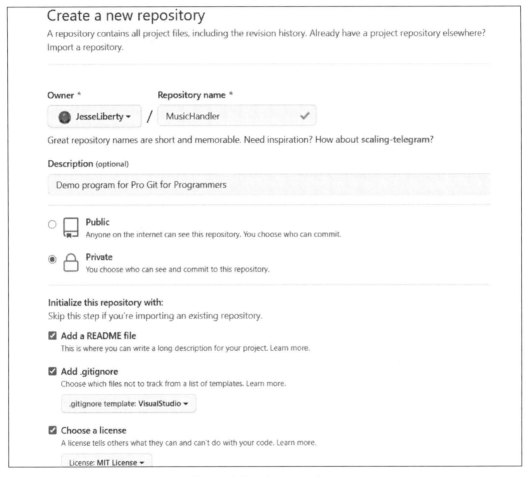

Figure 6.1: Creating a repository

With the repository created, we need to clone it into a local repository. This time let's use Visual Studio, and GitHub's awareness of Visual Studio. On GitHub click on **Code** and when the dropdown opens, choose **Open with Visual Studio**:

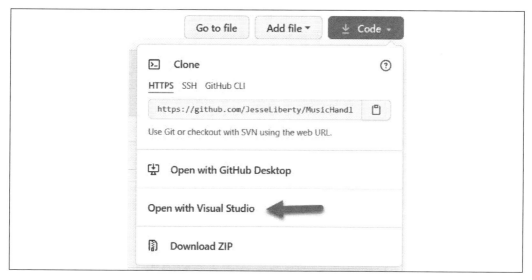

Figure 6.2: Downloading a commit with Visual Studio

When you do, Visual Studio will open and offer to save your project, with the name and default location chosen. For this exercise, create a solution with that project, and then add a `Music` class:

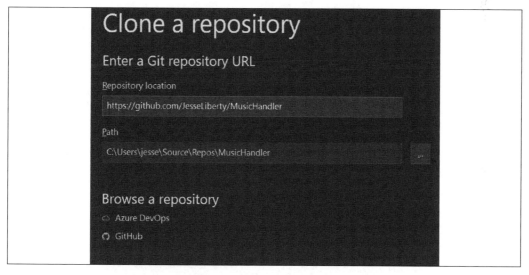

Figure 6.3: Cloning a repository with Visual Studio

Click on **Clone** in the lower-right corner and you will be brought to your application. You may be asked to sign in to GitHub if you haven't already done so from Visual Studio.

Because the checkboxes were selected at repo creation, your three files are already in the **Solution Explorer** (README.md, LICENSE, and .gitignore). Your next step is to create a project in that solution. In our case, we'll create a console application named MusicHandler. Click on **File | New Project** and select **Console Application**. You'll be asked what framework you'd like to use. For this console application any will do; I'll choose .NET 5. Click on **Create** in the lower right-hand corner.

Your application is created, complete with Program.cs. Let's make this our first commit. Staying in Visual Studio, we can click on the **Git** menu item, and choose **Commit or Stash**:

Figure 6.4: Your first commit with Visual Studio

As soon as you select it, the right-hand window (where **Solution Explorer** is) will turn into a Git handler:

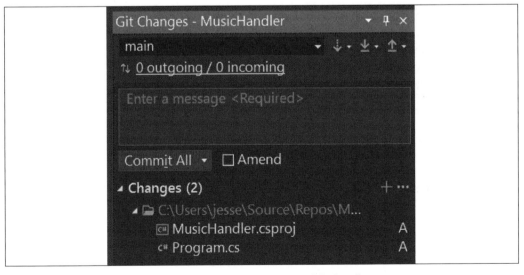

Figure 6.5: Visual Studio's principal Git handler

There is a lot of information here. At the bottom of the figure, you see that the project and `Program.cs` are marked as new (capital A) and that there are two changes (which is correct). You can stage them by clicking on the + sign. Or you can click on **Commit All** to both stage and commit your files.

Enter your message and select **Commit All**:

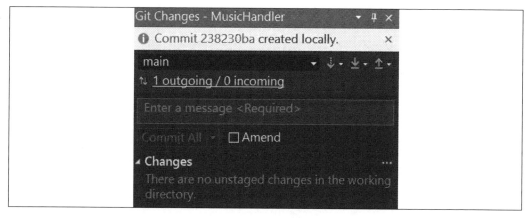

Figure 6.6: After creating a commit in Visual Studio

The view immediately changes in a few significant ways. At the top you see that a commit was created locally – that is, in the local repository. You also see that you now have "1 outgoing" – that is, one commit locally that has not been pushed to the server.

You also see an **Amend** checkbox; you can use that if you want to change the message on the most recent commit. Even though we have one outgoing, we are not going to push that commit. We need a number of local commits.

We need a solution to work with, so create a new project/solution in the same location. When you are done, your **Solution Explorer** should look like *Figure 6.7*:

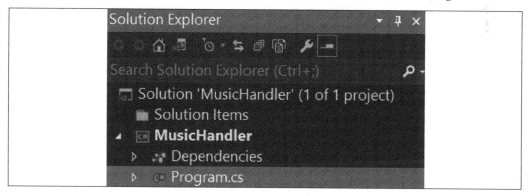

Figure 6.7: Creating a project in the repo folder

We're now ready to create our Music class:

```
using System;

public class Music
{
    public Music()
    {
    }
}
```

Let's commit that. You will see that your files are not yet tracked. You'll need to add them to the index:

```
git add .
```

Now you are ready to commit it:

```
git commit -m "Add music class"
```

If you look at the log, git log --oneline, you should see all three commits: the one created when you cloned the repository and the two you created by hand:

```
8147adb (HEAD -> main) Add music class
238230b Initial Commit
b6fc88f (origin/main, origin/HEAD) Initial commit
```

Let's create two more commits. We'll start by giving the Music class some properties, committing as we add each one:

```
using System;

public class Music
{
    public string Name { get; set; }
    public string Artist { get; set; }
    public DateTime ReleaseDate { get; set; }

}
```

We can review our commits by going to the **Git** menu and choosing **View Branch History** (which is much like git log --oneline):

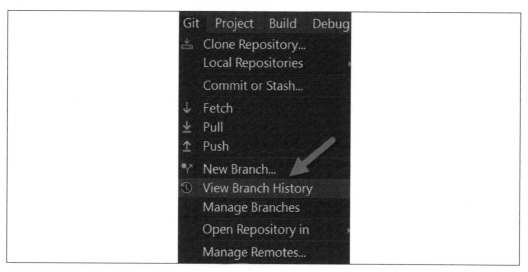

Figure 6.8: Reviewing a commit in Visual Studio

The result is a list of the IDs, the author of the commit, the date of the commit, and the commit message, as shown in *Figure 6.9*:

Figure 6.9: Reviewing the history of commits in Visual Studio

Notice that Visual Studio differentiates between those commits that are already on the server (under **Local History**) and those that have not yet been pushed (under **Outgoing**).

Let's add just three more commits. If you followed along, then you are as stuck as I am with Music outside of any namespace. Let's fix that:

```
using System;
namespace MusicHandler
{
```

```
    public class Music
    {
        public string Name { get; set; }
        public string Artist { get; set; }
        public DateTime ReleaseDate { get; set; }


    }
}
```

Now drag `Music.cs` out of the solution and into the project, and you will thus have fixed my error. This is an easy error to make when grabbing a solution from a repository using Visual Studio.

Commit these changes.

Now we can make an instance of `Music` inside `Program.cs` and commit that:

```
static void Main(string[] args)
{
    var music = new Music();
    music.Name = "Ripple";
    music.Artist = "Grateful Dead";
    music.ReleaseDate = new DateTime(11, 1, 1970);
}
```

We can now use the **Git** menu in Visual Studio to see the entire commit history:

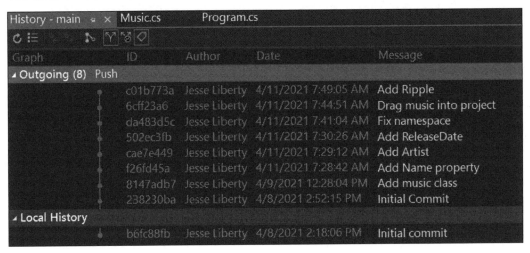

Figure 6.10: Returning to Visual Studio to see the entire commit history

We should see the same information in our log from the command line:

```
> git lg
* c01b773 - (HEAD → main) Add Ripple (4 minutes ago) <Jesse Liberty>
* 6cff23a - Drag music into project (8 minutes ago) <Jesse Liberty>
* da483d5 - Fix namespace (12 minutes ago) <Jesse Liberty>
* 502ec3f - Add ReleaseDate (22 minutes ago) <Jesse Liberty>
* cae7e44 - Add Artist (24 minutes ago) <Jesse Liberty>
* f26fd45 - Add Name property (24 minutes ago) <Jesse Liberty>
* 8147adb - Add music class (2 days ago) <Jesse Liberty>
* 238230b - Initial Commit (3 days ago) <Jesse Liberty>
* b6fc88f - (origin/main, origin/HEAD) Initial commit (3 days ago) <Jesse Liberty>
```

Figure 6.11: Using the log to see the commit history

Using interactive rebase to clean up your commits

Let us suppose that we do not want the three commits of name, artist, and release date to appear as separate commits, cluttering up the history. This is where interactive rebase comes in. We need only to count the number of commits down to one or two past the Add Name property. Let's say we decide on 7. We can then enter:

```
git rebase -i HEAD~7
```

Git will respond with:

```
hint: waiting for your editor to close the file...
```

and it will open Visual Studio Code as shown in *Figure 6.12*:

```
≡ git-rebase-todo ✕

C: > Users > jesse > source > repos > MusicHandler > .git > rebase-merge > ≡ git-rebase-todo
    1    pick 8147adb Add music class
    2    pick f26fd45 Add Name property
    3    pick cae7e44 Add Artist
    4    pick 502ec3f Add ReleaseDate
    5    pick da483d5 Fix namespace
    6    pick 6cff23a Drag music into project
    7    pick c01b773 Add Ripple
```

Figure 6.12: Waiting for your editor to open

Now comes the fun part. For each line, we have a number of options:

- Leave pick, which will just keep the commit as is
- Squash – the one we want, explained below
- Drop – leave that commit out – erase it
- Label – label chosen commit(s) with a label (see *Chapter 6, Using the Log*)

You can also re-order your commits if that is somehow helpful to you.

Let's do what we set out to do, squash the release, name, and artist into the commit above (create the music class). With Visual Studio Code make the changes shown in *Figure 6.13*:

```
pick 8147adb Add music class
s f26fd45 Add Name property
s cae7e44 Add Artist
s 502ec3f Add ReleaseDate
pick da483d5 Fix namespace
pick 6cff23a Drag music into project
pick c01b773 Add Ripple
```

Figure 6.13: Inside the editor for an interactive rebase

Notice we are set to squash the release date into the artist (making them one commit), then squash that commit into Name, and then take all of that and squash it into the music class. This will make one commit out of the four.

Save the file; Git comes back and re-opens the file and offers to allow you to fix up the messages. It starts by showing you what messages you had, as shown in *Figure 6.14*:

```
# This is a combination of 4 commits.
# This is the 1st commit message:
Add music class
# This is the commit message #2:
Add Name property
# This is the commit message #3:
Add Artist
# This is the commit message #4:
Add ReleaseDate
```

Figure 6.14: The history of the messages

You can now choose your message (and edit it as well) leaving out or including the previous messages.

I will choose one meaningful message:

```
# This is a combination of 4 commits.
# This is the 1st commit message:

Add music class
```

Figure 6.15: Choosing the messages you want to keep

Notice, again, that there are extensive comments at the bottom of the file to help you understand what is happening:

```
# interactive rebase in progress; onto 238230b
# Last commands done (4 commands done):
#    squash cae7e44 Add Artist
#    squash 502ec3f Add ReleaseDate
# Next commands to do (3 remaining commands):
#    pick da483d5 Fix namespace
#    pick 6cff23a Drag music into project
# You are currently rebasing branch 'main' on '238230b'.
#
```

Figure 6.16: Progress notes on your interactive feedback

When we save and close this file, Git tells us that the rebase was successful.

If you ask Git for the status at this point, you'll get a review of where your rebase stands:

```
Last commands done (4 commands done):
    squash cae7e44 Add Artist
    squash 502ec3f Add ReleaseDate
    (see more in file .git/rebase-merge/done)
Next commands to do (3 remaining commands):
    pick da483d5 Fix namespace
    pick 6cff23a Drag music into project
    (use "git rebase --edit-todo" to view and edit)
You are currently rebasing branch 'main' on '238230b'.
    (all conflicts fixed: run "git rebase --continue")

Changes to be committed:
    (use "git restore --staged <file>..." to unstage)
        modified:   Music.cs
```

Figure 6.17: Git status after an interactive rebase

Enter git rebase --continue and you should see a recap and success message as shown in *Figure 6.18*:

```
1 file changed, 3 insertions(+), 5 deletions(-)
Successfully rebased and updated refs/heads/main.
```

Figure 6.18: Git summary of interactive rebase

Your rebase worked. Let's look at the log:

```
git lg
    - (HEAD -> main) Add Ripple (3 minutes ago) <Jesse Liberty>
    - Drag music into project (3 minutes ago) <Jesse Liberty>
    - Fix namespace (3 minutes ago) <Jesse Liberty>
    - Add music class (3 minutes ago) <Jesse Liberty>
    - # This is a combination of 3 commits. # This is the 1st commit message: (13 minutes ago) <Jesse Liberty>
    - Initial Commit (3 days ago) <Jesse Liberty>
    - (origin/main, origin/HEAD) Initial commit (3 days ago) <Jesse Liberty>
```

Figure 6.19: Log reflects the interactive rebase

Let's turn back to Visual Studio and ask for a history:

▲ Outgoing (6) Push					
	be3e5021	Jesse Liberty	4/11/2021 7:49:05 AM	Add Ripple
	aa2824cc	Jesse Liberty	4/11/2021 7:44:51 AM	Drag music into project
	2b203071	Jesse Liberty	4/11/2021 7:41:04 AM	Fix namespace
	817b28e4	Jesse Liberty	4/11/2021 7:30:26 AM	Add music class
	d27ecd0b	Jesse Liberty	4/9/2021 12:28:04 PM	# This is a combination of 3 commits.
	238230ba	Jesse Liberty	4/8/2021 2:52:15 PM	Initial Commit
▲ Local History					
	b6fc88fb	Jesse Liberty	4/8/2021 2:18:06 PM	Initial commit

Figure 6.20: Looking at the modified history in Visual Studio

Notice that the interim commits are gone! They have been merged into **Add music class**.

Interactive rebase is both powerful and safe. It can clean up your commits before pushing them, making it easier for your teammates to read the history. If you get into trouble during the interaction with interactive rebase, you can enter:

```
--abort
```

to return to where you were before the interactive rebase started.

I confess, I use squash all the time, and I almost never use any of the other options; though it is good to know they are there.

Summary

In this chapter you learned:

- How to use interactive rebase to squash commits before pushing them
- Other options in interactive rebase
- The impact of squash in interactive rebase
- How to fix up the messages for your rebased files

Challenge

In this challenge you will create a new project that you will clone to your local repository using GitHub Desktop. You will then add at least 7-8 commits. Finally, you'll use interactive rebase to squash some of your commits together. Feel free to experiment with some of the other options in interactive rebase.

For my project I'm going to create a solution that tracks the Rocky Horror Picture Show (a true classic).

Step 1, as usual, is to create the new repository:

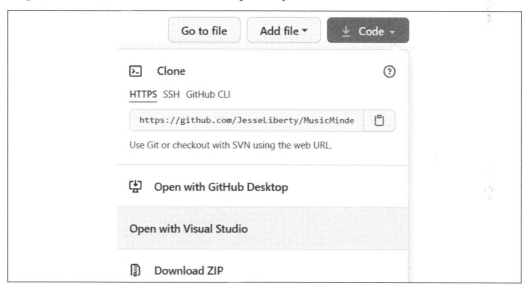

Figure 6.21: Creating the repo

Step 2 is to clone to your disk; however, this time we'll use GitHub Desktop:

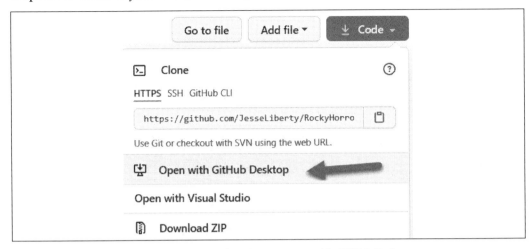

Figure 6.22: Downloading the repository with GitHub Desktop

GitHub Desktop will be launched:

Launching GitHub Desktop...

If nothing happens, download GitHub Desktop and try again.

Go back

Figure 6.23: Launching GitHub Desktop

GitHub Desktop will launch and pop up a modal dialog box asking you to confirm or change the repository and where you want to put it on your disk:

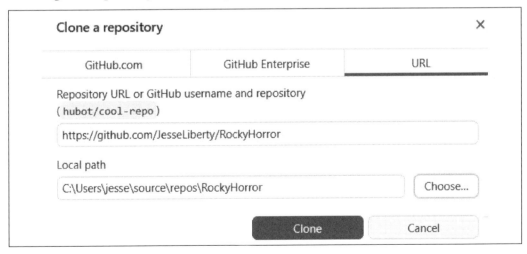

Figure 6.24: Cloning to GitHub Desktop

As expected, your repository is cloned to the folder you designated, and GitHub Desktop is set to your repository and main branch:

Figure 6.25: Confirming the local repository was created

The next step is to create a project in that directory. GitHub Desktop is immediately populated on the left side with the files you've entered, and on the right side with the changes to the selected file:

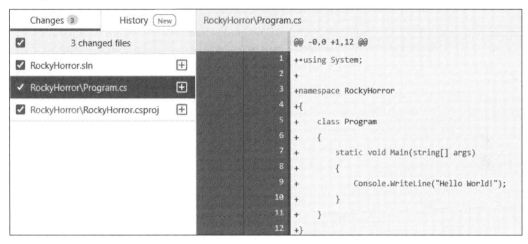

Figure 6.26: Creating a project in your repository directory

We want to commit this, but not push it. We make the commit using the commit section at the bottom left:

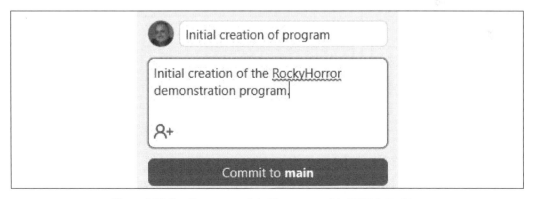

Figure 6.27: Creating a commit (with a message) in GitHub Desktop

GitHub Desktop reconfigures to show you the current state of your project:

Figure 6.28: The state of your project, shown in GitHub Desktop

Following the arrows from left to right we see that there are now zero changes to report; this is reiterated in the headline and the third arrow points to the button that would push your changes to origin (which we will not do now).

In the upper left-hand corner is a button that says **History**; clicking that brings you to your commit history, with each file added or modified in that commit listed:

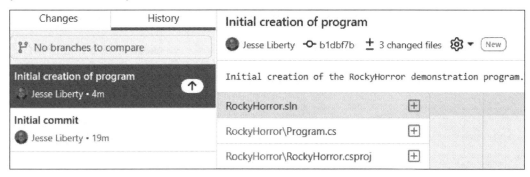

Figure 6.29: Your commit history in GitHub Desktop

There is quite a bit to see here. The highlighted commit has an up arrow offering to push it to origin. It also has the one-line headline from the commit, which is repeated on the right where you will also find the commit message. Once again, clicking on any of the files in that commit will show the changes in the right-hand window (not shown).

Now let's add commits as we have in the past. I opted to begin by creating a class called Showing, which will have properties for the location and time of each showing of the film in Boston for a given week:

```
namespace RockyHorror
{
    public class Showing
    {
    }
}
```

I'll commit after creating the class and each of its properties. When I'm done, Showing looks like this:

```
namespace RockyHorror
{
    public class Showing
    {
        public string Location { get; set; }
        public int NumberOfSeats { get; set; }
        public List<DateTime> ShowTimes { get; set; }
    }
}
```

The first time I saved this file, ShowTimes was just a DateTime, but I quickly realized that would require an object at each location for each showtime, so I changed it to a list of DateTime objects.

Program.cs ended up looking like this:

```
using System;
using System.Collections.Generic;

namespace RockyHorror
{
    class Program
    {
        static void Main(string[] args)
        {
            var showing = new Showing();
            showing.Location = "Brattle";
            showing.NumberOfSeats = 250;
            showing.ShowTimes = new List<DateTime>
            {
                new DateTime(0,0,0,10,0,0),
                new DateTime(0,0,0,13,0,0),
                new DateTime(0,0,0,16,0,0),
```

```
            new DateTime(0,0,0,19,0,0),
            new DateTime(0,0,0,22,0,0),
            new DateTime(0,0,0,0,0,1)
        };
    }
  }
}
```

The first time I committed the ShowTimes I forgot to include midnight (horrors!). Let's look at the history available in GitHub Desktop:

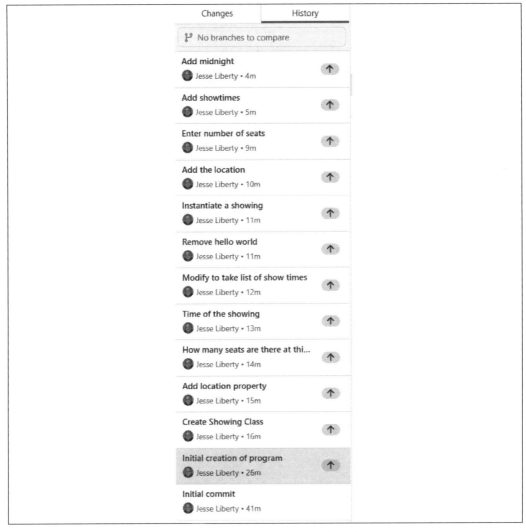

Figure 6.30: Commit history in GitHub Desktop

Before we push these, let's clean them up with an interactive rebase. We can combine some commits, and more interesting, we can drop the commit with just a single time because it is replaced with the commit that makes ShowTimes into a list.

The easiest way to do so is to use the command line to bring up the editor.

Here is the initial state of our interactive rebase:

```
pick b1dbf7b Initial creation of program
pick 98b26f9 Create Showing Class
pick 04ceafe Add location property
pick 32495b0 How many seats are there at this location
pick 1207db1 Time of the showing
pick ad35c32 Modify to take list of show times
pick 69837b7 Remove hello world
pick b78229e Instantiate a showing
pick 1516f7b Add the location
pick 0768ee0 Enter number of seats
pick 3fb0eda Add showtimes
pick 70d0373 Add midnight
```

Figure 6.31: Before the interactive rebase

And here is where we'll end up:

```
pick b1dbf7b Initial creation of program
pick 98b26f9 Create Showing Class
pick 04ceafe Add location property
pick 32495b0 How many seats are there at this location
d 1207db1 Time of the showing
pick ad35c32 Modify to take list of show times
pick 69837b7 Remove hello world
pick b78229e Instantiate a showing
s 1516f7b Add the location
s 0768ee0 Enter number of seats
s 3fb0eda Add showtimes
s 70d0373 Add midnight
```

Figure 6.32: After the interactive rebase

We are dropping the commit in which showtime was a DateTime as it is replaced by the next commit where ShowTimes is a list of DateTime objects. We are also squashing all the entries into our instance into a single commit. Once we save this, we will have an opportunity to fix up the messages.

Oops, we are notified there is a conflict:

```
error: could not apply ad35c32... Modify to take list of show times
Resolve all conflicts manually, mark them as resolved with
"git add/rm <conflicted_files>", then run "git rebase --continue".
You can instead skip this commit: run "git rebase --skip".
To abort and get back to the state before "git rebase", run "git rebase --abort".
Could not apply ad35c32... Modify to take list of show times
Auto-merging RockyHorror/Showing.cs
CONFLICT (content): Merge conflict in RockyHorror/Showing.cs
```

Figure 6.33: A conflict during the interactive rebase

Git offers us a number of alternatives: fix the conflict and then continue the rebase or skip the conflicted commit and abort the rebase. Let's fix the problem by returning to GitHub Desktop:

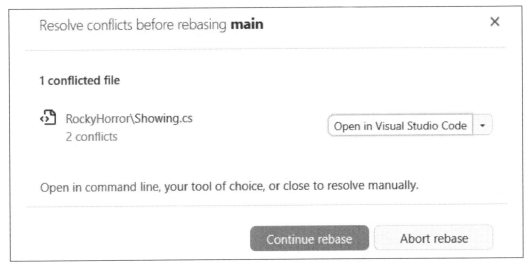

Figure 6.34: Finding the conflict in GitHub Desktop

Notice that GitHub Desktop knows about the conflict too, and offers a number of choices:

- Open in Visual Studio Code
- Open in the command line
- Open with your tool of choice
- Resolve manually

Let's choose to open in Visual Studio Code:

```
C: > Users > jesse > source > repos > RockyHorror > RockyHorror > C Showing.cs
      Accept Current Change | Accept Incoming Change | Accept Both Changes | Compare Changes
 1  <<<<<<< HEAD (Current Change)
 2  namespace RockyHorror
 3  =======
 4  using System;
 5  using System.Collections.Generic;
 6
 7  namespace RockyHorror
 8  >>>>>>> ad35c32 (Modify to take list of show times) (Incoming Change)
 9  {
10      public class Showing
11      {
12          public string Location { get; set; }
13          public int NumberOfSeats { get; set; }
      Accept Current Change | Accept Incoming Change | Accept Both Changes | Compare Changes
14  <<<<<<< HEAD (Current Change)
15  =======
16          public List<DateTime> ShowTimes { get; set; }
17  >>>>>>> ad35c32 (Modify to take list of show times) (Incoming Change)
18      }
19  }
```

Figure 6.35: The conflict in Visual Studio

Visual Studio Code works hard to help you make the changes. Notice the small menus that allow you to accept one or the other or both changes (and it gives you the message on the incoming change to make sure you know what you are choosing). When you are done, the file looks as you intended:

```
using System;
using System.Collections.Generic;

namespace RockyHorror
{
    public class Showing
    {
        public string Location { get; set; }
        public int NumberOfSeats { get; set; }
        public List<DateTime> ShowTimes { get; set; }
    }
}
```

Save and close the file. When you return to the command line, add the fixed file back in and then tell Git to continue:

```
git add .
git rebase --continue
```

Visual Studio Code will open again, to allow you to fix up the commit messages. Save and close and Visual Studio Code will open a third time to allow you to fix up all your messages. Once you save and close that, much to your relief, Git will tell you that the rebase has succeeded:

```
1 file changed, 13 insertions(+)
Successfully rebased and updated refs/heads/main.
```

Figure 6.36: Your interactive rebase worked!

7
Workflow, Notes, and Tags

In this chapter, we will see

- The standard workflow using Git
- What notes are
- How to use notes
- What tags are
- How to use tags

We'll start off by examining the standard workflow.

Standard workflow

The standard workflow is pretty much what we've seen in the previous five chapters, except that you usually would not commit so quickly or often. Typically, it goes like this:

1. Create a repository.
2. Either clone that repository from the server, or if it was created locally, push it to the server.
3. Create a branch.
4. Code.
5. Test.
6. Commit.
7. Repeat *steps 4-6* until you have a block of code that does "something" (e.g. opens a dialog box and processes the result).

8. Test.

9. Commit.

10. Push.

11. Repeat *steps 4-10* until you have fulfilled a requirement (self-imposed or otherwise).

12. Merge into the main branch (or create a pull request if you are in a team).

There are variants on this. Some people like to push after each commit, but that prevents them from using interactive rebase to reorganize their commits. What happens though if you have pushed your commit and realize that there is additional information you wish you had added to the message?

Do *not* modify code you've pushed. (Have I said that before?) So, what to do?

If the problem is significant (you need to modify the commit contents, etc.) then you'll need to take more drastic measures (see *Chapter 12, Fixing Mistakes* on fixing mistakes). But if it is just a matter of updating the message, consider adding a note.

Mirroring your repo

We want to go on to discuss notes, but to do so we need to take a digression into mirroring our repository so that we can add notes without messing up our existing repo.

The repository we want to mirror should have a fair number of commits. You may remember from the previous chapter that I answered the challenge by creating a repository called RockyHorror. Let's open that repo on our local machine and use the log to see the commits:

```
$ git log --oneline
e16d191 (HEAD -> main, origin/main, origin/HEAD) Add program.cs first modifications
f55eb4e Instantiate a showing
bb4927c Remove hello world
bf6b900 Enter show times
32495b0 How many seats are there at this location
04ceafe Add location property
98b26f9 Create Showing Class
b1dbf7b Initial creation of program
d396657 Initial commit
```

Figure 7.1: What's in the existing repository?

 Note: You are not going crazy: for this chapter I've switched from PowerShell to the Bash shell.

Replicating an existing repo

As you can see there are nine commits, which will be enough for our purposes. However, I don't want to modify this repository (principally so that when you download the code it will look right when you are reading *Chapter 6, Interactive Rebasing*).

To get an exact copy of this repository into another, complete with commits, messages, etc., we're going to use Git's --mirror flag. Here's how you do it.

Change directory to RockyHorror and make sure you are in the local repository by using the log, using the --oneline flag, as shown previously in *Figure 7.1*.

Now, we need a repository to put our mirrored version into. Go to GitHub and create a new repository named RockyHorror2:

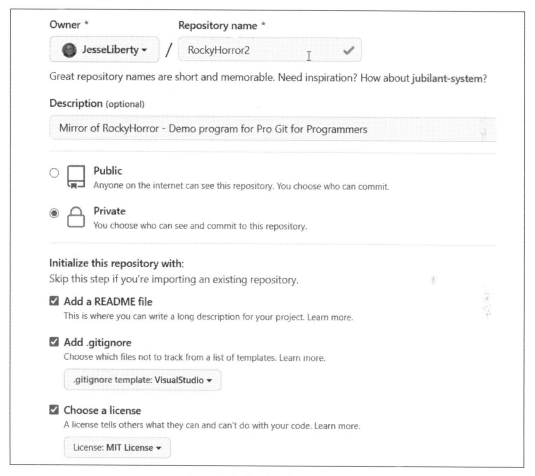

Figure 7.2: Creating the new repo

As you would expect, you now have a repository, RockyHorror2, on the server but not locally. We are now going to overwrite the files, commits, etc. on the server with the contents of RockyHorror, giving us an exact duplicate to work with.

To do this, make sure you are in the original repository (RockyHorror), and then push to the server using the --mirror flag and pushing to the new repository (RockyHorror2). You'll need the address of your new repo, so start by going to the clone button on the server and copying the address, but *do not clone the repo*:

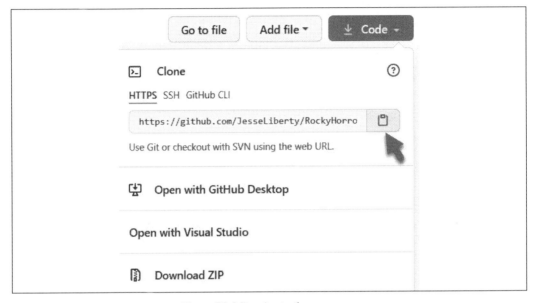

Figure 7.3: Mirroring to the new repo

Okay, let's review. In your terminal (Bash, PowerShell, Terminal, etc.) you are in the directory for RockyHorror and if you call git log --oneline you will get the results shown in *Figure 7.1*.

Now you are ready to mirror this repo locally. You'll do that from your terminal, but remember, what it is going to do is push a mirror of this repository onto the server, overwriting whatever is already in RockyHorror2 (in this case just the README.md, the LICENSE, and the .gitignore file).

This will cause Git to take a number of actions, the net effect of which is to copy everything from RockyHorror over to RockyHorror2:

```
$ git push --mirror https://github.com/JesseLiberty/RockyHorror2.git
Enumerating objects: 39, done.
Counting objects: 100% (39/39), done.
Delta compression using up to 8 threads
Compressing objects: 100% (39/39), done.
Writing objects: 100% (39/39), 7.53 KiB | 1.88 MiB/s, done.
Total 39 (delta 18), reused 4 (delta 0), pack-reused 0
remote: Resolving deltas: 100% (18/18), done.
To https://github.com/JesseLiberty/RockyHorror2.git
 + f982b74...e16d191 main -> main (forced update)
 * [new reference]   origin/HEAD -> origin/HEAD
 * [new reference]   origin/main -> origin/main
```

Figure 7.4: Copying from the server to a local repo

You can now go to GitHub and see that RockyHorror2 has been updated to be an exact replica of RockyHorror (If you don't see that, remember to refresh the page):

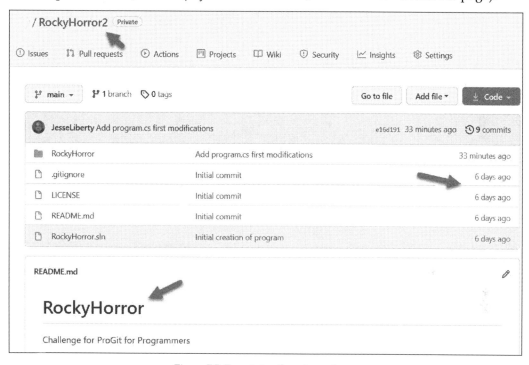

Figure 7.5: Examining the mirrored repo

There are a few interesting things to see in *Figure 7.5*. First, notice in the upper left that we're in RockyHorror2, but if you look at the README it says RockyHorror. That is because that README came from the original RockyHorror repo. Also notice that the files are not from a few minutes ago, but in my case from 6 days ago; that is because I modified those files 6 days ago in the original repo. The point, which really can be hard to wrap your head around, is that this is an exact duplicate of RockyHorror.

Now go to RockyHorror2 on your local machine. What? It isn't there? Right, we only mirrored to the server. If we want a local repository we need to clone our new one. You can do that using the command line, Visual Studio, or GitHub Desktop as we've seen (or any other GUI you like. SourceTree and Fork are very popular as of the time of writing).

When you are cloning, make sure you copy the address of the new repo, not the original:

```
jesse@Win10 MINGW64 /c/users/jesse/source/repos
$ git clone https://github.com/JesseLiberty/RockyHorror2.git
Cloning into 'RockyHorror2'...
remote: Enumerating objects: 39, done.
remote: Counting objects: 100% (39/39), done.
remote: Compressing objects: 100% (21/21), done.
remote: Total 39 (delta 18), reused 39 (delta 18), pack-reused 0
Receiving objects: 100% (39/39), 7.53 KiB | 1.51 MiB/s, done.
Resolving deltas: 100% (18/18), done.
```

Figure 7.6: Ensuring you are in the right place

You now can change into the new RockyHorror2 directory. Do so and get a log of what is in there:

```
jesse@Win10 MINGW64 /c/users/jesse/source/repos/RockyHorror2 (main)
$ git log --oneline
e16d191 (HEAD -> main, origin/main, origin/HEAD) Add program.cs first modifications
f55eb4e Instantiate a showing
bb4927c Remove hello world
bf6b900 Enter show times
32495b0 How many seats are there at this location
04ceafe Add location property
98b26f9 Create Showing Class
b1dbf7b Initial creation of program
d396657 Initial commit
```

Figure 7.7: Getting a log of the mirrored repo

A key thing to notice here is that the commits and where HEAD and origin are pointing to are identical to RockyHorror as shown in *Figure 7.1*.

Notice that the ID is identical as well. I personally find this almost shocking, but as far as Git is concerned this is just another copy of the same repo. From now on, however, you can change one without affecting the other.

Adding and showing notes

Now we are ready to add a note to one of our commits.

 Let me be clear, you do *not* have to mirror your repo to use notes. We only did that here for the purposes of the book; to ensure that the repos correspond to what is shown in each chapter. Normally, you would just add the note.

Notes are just bits of text you can attach to a commit after it is already in the repo. A common use for notes is to explain how a commit fits in with other commits, or perhaps to flag a commit for amending or rebasing, or really to add any information you want to paste onto the commit. It does not change the commit; it is like a post-it you tack on.

To add the note, you'll use the git notes command with one or more flags. For example, if you have the code in *Figure 7.7* and you want to add a note to the commit that currently says "Remove Hello World" all we need to do is to get the ID commit id–bb4927c– and execute like this:

```
git notes add -m "Remove from program.cs" bb4927c
```

If you now run git log you'll see the note in the log listing, prefixed by the word Notes:

```
commit bb4927ca00fbcbd2c9ec2dfd01e049ace670182c
Author: Jesse Liberty <jesseliberty@gmail.com>
Date:   Mon Apr 12 08:37:49 2021 -0400

    Remove hello world

Notes:
    Remove from program.cs
```

Figure 7.8: Seeing the attached note

If you want to see your changes along with the note, use the show subcommand:

```
jesse@Win10 MINGW64 /c/users/jesse/source/repos/RockyHorror2 (main)
$ git show bb4927c
commit bb4927ca00fbcbd2c9ec2dfd01e049ace670182c
Author: Jesse Liberty <jesseliberty@gmail.com>
Date:   Mon Apr 12 08:37:49 2021 -0400

    Remove hello world

Notes:
    Remove from program.cs

diff --git a/RockyHorror/Program.cs b/RockyHorror/Program.cs
index 2f50edf..ec9d563 100644
--- a/RockyHorror/Program.cs
+++ b/RockyHorror/Program.cs
@@ -6,7 +6,6 @@ namespace RockyHorror
     {
         static void Main(string[] args)
         {
             Console.WriteLine("Hello World!");
         }
     }
}
```

Figure 7.9: Seeing your changes with the notes

Once again, there are many subcommands that you can Google for when the need arises.

Tags

It can be convenient to mark a given commit with a name. For example, you might mark one commit as the developer release, and another as the general release. Each time you make a new release you add another tag, giving you a quick and clean way to look through the history and see which commits were added before or after each release.

Let's look back at *Figure 7.1* one more time. We might decide that the commit Enter show times is the last commit in creating the Show object, and we'd like to indicate that. We can do so with a note, but in this case, it may be more convenient to tag that commit.

There are two types of tags you might use: a simple tag and an annotated tag. Let's start with a simple tag:

```
jesse@Win10 MINGW64 /c/users/jesse/source/repos/RockyHorror2 (main)
$ git log --oneline
e16d191 (HEAD -> main, origin/main, origin/HEAD) Add program.cs first modifications
f55eb4e Instantiate a showing
bb4927c Remove hello world
bf6b900 Enter show times
32495b0 How many seats are there at this location
04ceafe Add location property
98b26f9 Create Showing Class
b1dbf7b Initial creation of program
d396657 Initial commit

jesse@Win10 MINGW64 /c/users/jesse/source/repos/RockyHorror2 (main)
$ git tag LastShowCommit bf6b900

jesse@Win10 MINGW64 /c/users/jesse/source/repos/RockyHorror2 (main)
$ git log --oneline
e16d191 (HEAD -> main, origin/main, origin/HEAD) Add program.cs first modifications
f55eb4e Instantiate a showing
bb4927c Remove hello world
bf6b900 (tag: LastShowCommit) Enter show times
32495b0 How many seats are there at this location
04ceafe Add location property
98b26f9 Create Showing Class
b1dbf7b Initial creation of program
d396657 Initial commit

jesse@Win10 MINGW64 /c/users/jesse/source/repos/RockyHorror2 (main)
$ |
```

Figure 7.10: Tag for LastShowCommit

In *Figure 7.10* we first take an online log of all the commits. We then add the tag:

```
git tag LastShowCommit bf6b900
```

As you can see, we use the keyword `tag` followed by the tag itself (one word, no quotes) followed by the ID of the commit we're tagging.

Note that we are tagging a commit, not a given file. This tag applies to all the files in that commit.

The second type of tag is an annotated tag, as shown in *Figure 7.11*:

```
jesse@Win10 MINGW64 /c/users/jesse/source/repos/RockyHorror2 (main)
$ git tag -a TestOfShowObject f55eb4e -m "Mark switch to testing the show object"
```

Figure 7.11: Annotated tag

When you use the oneline log, this appears just as the other tag did, as shown in *Figure 7.12:*

```
jesse@win10 MINGW64 /c/users/jesse/source/repos/RockyHorror2 (main)
$ git log --oneline
e16d191 (HEAD -> main, origin/main, origin/HEAD) Add program.cs first modifications
f55eb4e (tag: TestOfShowObject) Instantiate a showing
bb4927c Remove hello world
bf6b900 (tag: LastShowCommit) Enter show times
32495b0 How many seats are there at this location
04ceafe Add location property
98b26f9 Create Showing Class
b1dbf7b Initial creation of program
d396657 Initial commit
```

Figure 7.12: Annotated tag in the oneline log

If, however, you use the show command, you can see the tag with the additional information you supplied (i.e. the message) when it was created and by whom. It is very similar to a commit, except that no files are affected, and it is marked with the keywords **tag** and **tagger**:

```
$ git show TestOfShowObject
tag TestOfShowObject
Tagger: Jesse Liberty <jesseliberty@gmail.com>
Date:   Sun Apr 18 17:26:01 2021 -0400

Mark switch to testing the show object

commit f55eb4ea8fd025415968b5892c0150d6a6a35873 (tag: TestOfShowObject)
Author: Jesse Liberty <jesseliberty@gmail.com>
Date:   Mon Apr 12 08:38:32 2021 -0400

    Instantiate a showing

diff --git a/RockyHorror/Program.cs b/RockyHorror/Program.cs
index ec9d563..a3585d4 100644
--- a/RockyHorror/Program.cs
+++ b/RockyHorror/Program.cs
@@ -1,4 +1,5 @@
 using System;
+using System.Collections.Generic;

 namespace RockyHorror
 {
@@ -6,6 +7,18 @@ namespace RockyHorror
     {
         static void Main(string[] args)
         {
+            var showing = new Showing();
+            showing.Location = "Brattle";
+            showing.NumberOfSeats = 250;
+            showing.ShowTimes = new List<DateTime>
+            {
+                new DateTime(0,0,0,10,0,0),
+                new DateTime(0,0,0,13,0,0),
+                new DateTime(0,0,0,16,0,0),
+                new DateTime(0,0,0,19,0,0),
+                new DateTime(0,0,0,22,0,0),
+                new DateTime(0,0,0,0,0,1)
+            };
         }
     }
 }
```

Figure 7.13: The annotated tag

Pointing to a different tag

If you create a tag but point it to the wrong commit, you can change what it points to by using the force flag. For example, suppose you have the list of commits shown in *Figure 7.14*:

```
$ git log --oneline
e16d191 (HEAD -> main, origin/main, origin/HEAD) Add program.cs first modifications
f55eb4e (tag: TestOfShowObject) Instantiate a showing
bb4927c Remove hello world
bf6b900 (tag: LastShowCommit) Enter show times
32495b0 How many seats are there at this location
04ceafe Add location property
98b26f9 Create Showing Class
b1dbf7b Initial creation of program
d396657 Initial commit
```

Figure 7.14: List with tag at the wrong commit

Notice that the tag `TestOfShowObject` is pointing to `f55eb4e`. Unfortunately, we meant to point it to the next commit (`e16d191`). To do this, we can write:

```
git tag -f TestOfShowObject e16d191
```

We need the force flag (`-f`) to ensure that Git doesn't complain with `Fatal: tag TestOfShowObjects` already exists:

```
jesse@Win10 MINGW64 /c/users/jesse/source/repos/RockyHorror2 (main)
$ git tag -f TestOfShowObject e16d191
Updated tag 'TestOfShowObject' (was 3d0dc4b)

jesse@Win10 MINGW64 /c/users/jesse/source/repos/RockyHorror2 (main)
$ git log --oneline
e16d191 (HEAD -> main, tag: TestOfShowObject, origin/main, origin/HEAD) Add program
.cs first modifications
f55eb4e Instantiate a showing
bb4927c Remove hello world
bf6b900 (tag: LastShowCommit) Enter show times
32495b0 How many seats are there at this location
04ceafe Add location property
98b26f9 Create Showing Class
b1dbf7b Initial creation of program
d396657 Initial commit
```

Figure 7.15: Using the force command to reassign the tag

As you can see in *Figure 7.15*, Git responds with the message updated tag, the name of the tag, and what it had been pointing to. The tag has now been moved to `e16d191`, as we hoped.

Finally, we can delete a tag with the -d flag:

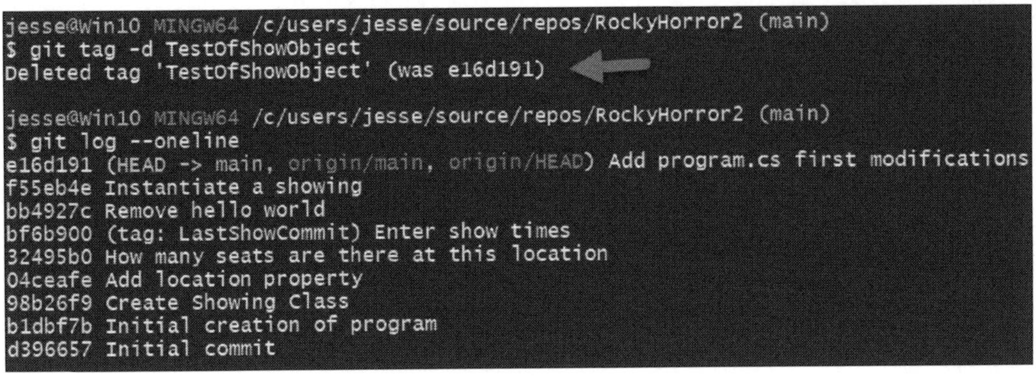

```
jesse@Win10 MINGW64 /c/users/jesse/source/repos/RockyHorror2 (main)
$ git tag -d TestOfShowObject
Deleted tag 'TestOfShowObject' (was e16d191)  ⬅

jesse@Win10 MINGW64 /c/users/jesse/source/repos/RockyHorror2 (main)
$ git log --oneline
e16d191 (HEAD -> main, origin/main, origin/HEAD) Add program.cs first modifications
f55eb4e Instantiate a showing
bb4927c Remove hello world
bf6b900 (tag: LastShowCommit) Enter show times
32495b0 How many seats are there at this location
04ceafe Add location property
98b26f9 Create Showing Class
b1dbf7b Initial creation of program
d396657 Initial commit
```

Figure 7.16: Deleting the tag

Figure 7.16 shows that Git confirms the deletion and running the log shows that the tag is gone.

Summary

In this chapter you learned

- The standard workflow using Git
- What notes are and how to create them
- What tags are and how to create, move, and delete them

Challenge

Create a local copy of `Panofy`. Add a note to one of the commits and ensure it is there. Add a tag to one of the commits and make sure it is there. Finally, change which commit the tag is pointing to.

Here is my answer:

First, switch directory to `Panofy`. If it is not on your local machine, clone it:

```
jesse@Win10 MINGW64 /c/users/jesse/source/repos
$ cd panofy
bash: cd: panofy: No such file or directory

jesse@Win10 MINGW64 /c/users/jesse/source/repos
$ git clone https://github.com/JesseLiberty/Panofy.git
Cloning into 'Panofy'...
remote: Enumerating objects: 50, done.
remote: Counting objects: 100% (50/50), done.
remote: Compressing objects: 100% (36/36), done.
remote: Total 50 (delta 24), reused 36 (delta 14), pack-reused 0
Receiving objects: 100% (50/50), 8.51 KiB | 670.00 KiB/s, done.
Resolving deltas: 100% (24/24), done.
```

Figure 7.17: Switching to the Panofy project

As shown in *Figure 7.17* when I tried to change directory to Panofy I was told it doesn't exist, so I cloned it from the server.

To create a mirror I first create a new repo on the server named Panofy2:

Figure 7.18: Mirroring

As you can see in *Figure 7.18*, this time I did not bother creating a license file as all of this will be overwritten when I mirror Panofy over it. To do so I change directory to Panofy (the original repo) and enter:

```
git push --mirror https://github.com/JesseLiberty/Panofy2.git
```

This takes the repository I'm in (`Panofy`) and pushes it to the new address, mirroring the original:

```
$ git push --mirror https://github.com/JesseLiberty/Panofy2.git
Enumerating objects: 50, done.
Counting objects: 100% (50/50), done.
Delta compression using up to 8 threads
Compressing objects: 100% (26/26), done.
Writing objects: 100% (50/50), 8.51 KiB | 4.26 MiB/s, done.
Total 50 (delta 24), reused 50 (delta 24), pack-reused 0
remote: Resolving deltas: 100% (24/24), done.
To https://github.com/JesseLiberty/Panofy2.git
 + 96570a3...4b080ba main -> main (forced update)
 * [new reference]   origin/HEAD -> origin/HEAD
 * [new reference]   origin/main -> origin/main
```

Figure 7.19: Pushing to the mirrored repo on the server

I'll switch to `Panofy2` on the server, and sure enough, the license is now there (from `Panofy`) along with the `Panofy` folder as shown in *Figure 7.20*:

Figure 7.20: License for Panofy

With that in place, I can safely change `Panofy2`. The first task is to add a note. Let's start with a log so that we can see what we have:

```
jesse@Win10 MINGW64 /c/users/jesse/source/repos/panofy (main)
$ git log --oneline
4b080ba (HEAD -> main, origin/main, origin/HEAD) change name of csproj to correct
ame
8d47c04 add converter skeleton
2ca4ad9 add subtract method
877348c Update csproj
c507abf Add Hello message
3c9929c Sync'ing with B
2661adc fix conflicts
edd7b01 Initial files from DirA
da77c91 First use of Panofy in Dir B
a253788 Initial commit
```

Figure 7.21: Adding a note to a commit in the mirrored repo

Let's add a note to the commit with the message `Add Hello Message` that says
`Traditional first Hello World`:

```
jesse@Win10 MINGW64 /c/users/jesse/source/repos/panofy (main)
$ git notes add c507abf
hint: Waiting for your editor to close the file...
[main 2021-04-19T13:26:15.306Z] update#setState idle
(node:7156) electron: The default of contextIsolation is deprecated and will
nging from false to true in a future release of Electron.  See https://github
lectron/electron/issues/23506 for more information
(node:7156) electron: The default of contextIsolation is deprecated and will
nging from false to true in a future release of Electron.  See https://github
lectron/electron/issues/23506 for more information
```

Figure 7.22: Adding a note

In *Figure 7.22* we see that this time I did not add the note in the Git statement.
Instead I waited for the editor (in my case Visual Studio Code) to open and I put the
statement in there. When I closed the file the note was entered, as shown in *Figure
7.23*:

```
commit c507abff60ef529265136fb20f34da350625b6aa
Author: Jesse Liberty <JesseLiberty@non.se.com>
Date:    Mon Feb 22 11:20:24 2021 -0500

    Add Hello message

Notes:
    Traditional Hello World
```

Figure 7.23: Adding the note with an editor

Let's look at the log once more:

```
jesse@Win10 MINGW64 /c/users/jesse/source/repos/panofy (main)
$ git log --oneline
4b080ba (HEAD -> main, origin/main, origin/HEAD) change name of csproj to correct
ame
8d47c04 add converter skeleton
2ca4ad9 add subtract method
877348c Update csproj
c507abf Add Hello message
8c9929c Sync'ing with B
2661adc fix conflicts
edd7b01 Initial files from DirA
da77c91 First use of Panofy in Dir B
a253788 Initial commit
```

Figure 7.24: Examining the log

I'll add an annotated tag to the commit that says Update csproj:

```
jesse@Win10 MINGW64 /c/users/jesse/source/repos/panofy (main)
$ git tag -a ReleaseCandidate 877348c -m "Added release candidate tag to mark
ess"

jesse@Win10 MINGW64 /c/users/jesse/source/repos/panofy (main)
$ git show ReleaseCandidate
tag ReleaseCandidate
Tagger: Jesse Liberty <jesseliberty@gmail.com>
Date:   Mon Apr 19 09:34:39 2021 -0400

Added release candidate tag to mark progress

commit 877348c77d4bee7c1a4ca9b2169aed9650e612a6 (tag: ReleaseCandidate)
Author: Jesse Liberty <JesseLiberty@non.se.com>
Date:   Mon Feb 22 12:27:58 2021 -0500

    Update csproj

diff --git a/Panofy/Panofy/Panofy.csproj b/Panofy/Panofy/PanofyB.csproj
similarity index 100%
rename from Panofy/Panofy/Panofy.csproj
rename to Panofy/Panofy/PanofyB.csproj
diff --git a/Panofy/Panofy/Program.cs b/Panofy/Panofy/Program.cs
index aff8277..6c9797c 100644
--- a/Panofy/Panofy/Program.cs
+++ b/Panofy/Panofy/Program.cs
@@ -7,6 +7,7 @@ namespace Panofy
        static void Main(string[] args)
        {
            Console.WriteLine("Hello main branch!");
            Console.WriteLine("Another output line");
        }
    }
}
```

Figure 7.25: Examining an annotated tag

There are four arrows in *Figure 7.25*. The first points to the creation of the tag. The second shows you the tag name, the third shows you who the tagger (creator of the tag) was, and the final arrow points to the text of the tag itself.

Let's look at the log again, as shown in *Figure 7.26*:

```
jesse@win10 MINGW64 /c/users/jesse/source/repos/panofy (main)
$ git log --oneline
4b080ba (HEAD -> main, origin/main, origin/HEAD) change name of csproj to correct
ame
8d47c04 add converter skeleton
2ca4ad9 add subtract method
877348c (tag: ReleaseCandidate) Update csproj
c507abf Add Hello message
3c9929c Sync'ing with B
2661adc fix conflicts
edd7b01 Initial files from DirA
da77c91 First use of Panofy in Dir B
a253788 Initial commit
```

Figure 7.26: An annotated tag in the oneline log

We can see the tag at `877348c`, but it turns out we had forgotten to update `csproj` and fixed that at commit `4b080ba`. Let's move the tag there:

```
jesse@win10 MINGW64 /c/users/jesse/source/repos/panofy (main)
$ git tag -f ReleaseCandidate 4b080ba
Updated tag 'ReleaseCandidate' (was a89d2dd)

jesse@win10 MINGW64 /c/users/jesse/source/repos/panofy (main)
$ git log --oneline
4b080ba (HEAD -> main, tag: ReleaseCandidate, origin/main, origin/HEAD) change
 of csproj to correct name
8d47c04 add converter skeleton
2ca4ad9 add subtract method
877348c Update csproj
c507abf Add Hello message
3c9929c Sync'ing with B
2661adc fix conflicts
edd7b01 Initial files from DirA
da77c91 First use of Panofy in Dir B
a253788 Initial commit
```

Figure 7.27: Moving the tag

In this final figure, *Figure 7.27*, you can see that we have moved the tag `ReleaseCandidate` to `4b080ba` as intended.

8
Aliases

Stop working so hard! In this chapter, we will look at Git aliases, which greatly reduce the amount of typing you have to do. Aliases can be very simple, or they can take arguments and flags.

Aliases

Aliases they allow you to create shortcuts to `git` commands. For example, I have the alias `st`, which stands for status. Thus, I enter:

```
git st
```

and it is exactly as if I had entered:

```
git status
```

We'll get to more exciting and useful aliases in just a moment, but first let's look at how these are created. To create an alias:

- Enter `git`
- Enter the keyword `config`
- Enter the flag `--global`
- Enter the keyword `alias` followed by a period and then the alias itself
- Enter the command you are aliasing

This sounds more complicated than it is. For example, to create the st alias, I entered:

```
git config --global alias.st status
```

Of course, you don't have to use global. Your alternatives are system and local, but personally, I always use global because I'm the only one on this computer and I want it to always be available.

Here is a slightly more complicated alias that allows you to create a branch and check it out:

```
git config --global alias.bc checkout -b
```

The important thing to notice here is that your alias can take one or more flags.

I can never remember if it is bc or cb, so I made another alias to execute the same command:

```
git config --global alias.cb checkout -b
```

One alias I use a lot commits everything and waits for a message from me:

```
git config --global alias.cam commit -a -m
```

When I type git cam it commits everything along with the message I give it:

```
git cam "Here is my message"
```

Finally, here is my favorite alias:

```
git config –global alias.lg log --graph --pretty=format:'%Cred%h%Creset
-%C(yellow)%d%Creset %s %Cgreen(%cr) %C(yellow)<%an>%Creset' --abbrev-
commit
```

This offers me an alternative to log --oneline that gives much more information:

```
> git lg
* e16d191 - (HEAD -> main, origin/main, origin/HEAD) Add program.cs first modifications (6 days ago) <Jesse Liberty>
* f55eb4e - Instantiate a showing (12 days ago) <Jesse Liberty>
* bb4927c - Remove hello world (12 days ago) <Jesse Liberty>
* bf6b908 - (tag: LastShowCommit) Enter show times (12 days ago) <Jesse Liberty>
* 3249550 - How many seats are there at this location (12 days ago) <Jesse Liberty>
* 0ceafe - Add location property (12 days ago) <Jesse Liberty>
* 98b26f9 - Create Showing Class (12 days ago) <Jesse Liberty>
* b1dbf7b - Initial creation of program (12 days ago) <Jesse Liberty>
* d396657 - Initial commit (12 days ago) <Jesse Liberty>
```

Figure 8.1: git lg

Looking from left to right, we see the SHA followed by the commit message, then in parentheses we can see how long ago it was committed and then by whom. As seen on the fourth line, if there is a tag it is shown before the message, and the pointers (HEAD, for example) are shown first after the SHA.

Let's briefly take the alias apart: Each color is surrounded by %C and %Creset. Some display items are displayed using shortcuts such as %h, which displays the SHA. Thus, to show the SHA in red we have '%Cred%h%Creset.

All of this is stored in your global configuration file, which you can access by entering:

```
git config --edit --global
```

which opens the global configuration file in your editor. Here you will find a number of sections, one of which contains the aliases:

```
[user]
    name = Jesse Liberty
    email = jesseliberty@gmail.com
[alias]
    co = checkout
    bc = checkout
    cb = checkout
    st = status
    cam = commit -a -m
    lg = log –graph --pretty=format:'%Cred%h%Creset
-%C(yellow)%d%Creset %s %Cgreen(%cr) %C(yellow)<%an>%Creset' --abbrev-
commit
```

Notice that the aliases are there, but with a slightly different syntax. You can add aliases directly here if you like. (Note that the red underlining has no meaning. That is just Visual Studio Code pointing out that it does not recognize these terms.)

Take heed: if you are going to use more than one flag, you must put your alias in quotes, as shown in this line (you'll recognize it later in my answer to the challenge):

```
git config --global alias.nx  "log --name-only --oneline"
```

Summary

Aliases are a convenient way to shorten otherwise lengthy commands. You create an alias with this sequence:

- Enter git
- Enter the keyword config
- Enter the flag --global
- Enter the keyword alias followed by a period and then the alias itself
- Enter the command you are aliasing

You can access the configuration file directly with:

```
git config --edit --global
```

Aliases are simple, easy, and incredibly useful when working at the command line.

Challenge

Create an alias that replaces the following command:

```
git log --name-only --oneline
```

Answer

To do this, I will go to the command line and enter:

```
git config --global alias.nx  "log --name-only --oneline"
```

The double quotes are needed because you are using two flags on log.

The result of calling this command is shown in *Figure 8.2*:

```
> git nx
e16d191 (HEAD → main, origin/main, origin/HEAD) Add program.cs first modifications
RockyHorror/Program.cs
f55eb4e Instantiate a showing
RockyHorror/Program.cs
bb4927c Remove hello world
RockyHorror/Program.cs
bf6b900 (tag: LastShowCommit) Enter show times
RockyHorror/Showing.cs
32495b0 How many seats are there at this location
RockyHorror/Showing.cs
04ceafe Add location property
RockyHorror/Showing.cs
98b26f9 Create Showing Class
RockyHorror/Showing.cs
b1dbf7b Initial creation of program
```

Figure 8.2: Our new alias at work

Notice that each commit is there, represented on a single line and with only the SHA and message (except when there is a tag or pointers, as shown on line 1 and line 7 in *Figure 8.2*).

9

Using the Log

One of the most powerful commands in Git is log. You've already seen the log being used a bit in previous chapters, but now it is time to look at it in detail.

The log can show you when each commit was created, who created it, and other useful information about the commit, such as what changed in each file. You have great control over what is displayed, as you will see in this chapter.

Getting started with log

Let's quickly build another project and repository:

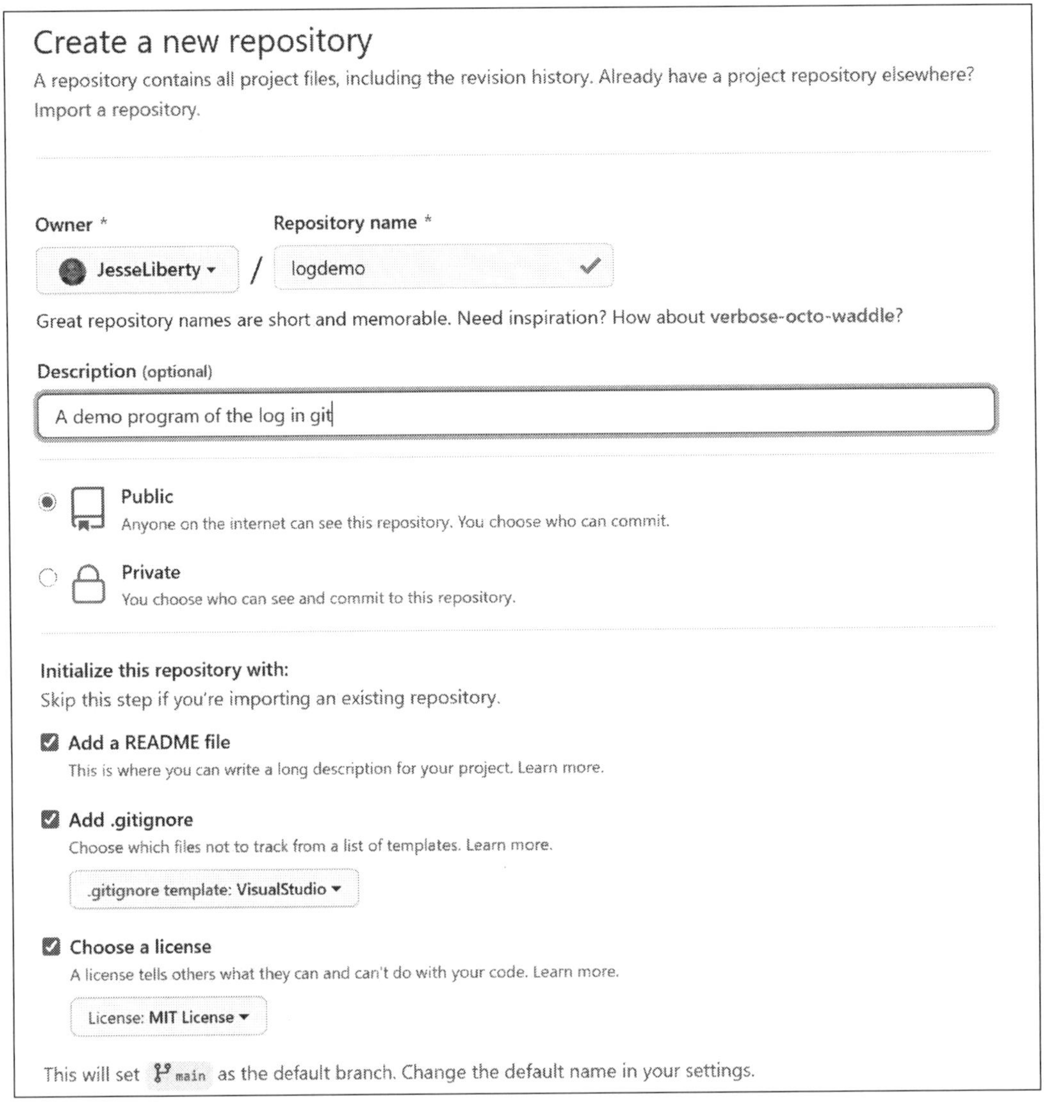

Create a new repository

A repository contains all project files, including the revision history. Already have a project repository elsewhere? Import a repository.

Owner * **Repository name** *

JesseLiberty ▾ / logdemo ✓

Great repository names are short and memorable. Need inspiration? How about **verbose-octo-waddle**?

Description (optional)

A demo program of the log in git

⦿ 📖 **Public**
Anyone on the internet can see this repository. You choose who can commit.

◯ 🔒 **Private**
You choose who can see and commit to this repository.

Initialize this repository with:
Skip this step if you're importing an existing repository.

☑ **Add a README file**
This is where you can write a long description for your project. Learn more.

☑ **Add .gitignore**
Choose which files not to track from a list of templates. Learn more.

.gitignore template: **VisualStudio** ▾

☑ **Choose a license**
A license tells others what they can and can't do with your code. Learn more.

License: **MIT License** ▾

This will set ⑂ main as the default branch. Change the default name in your settings.

Figure 9.1: Create a new repository

Next, as we have done before, we'll clone this repository to our local machine:

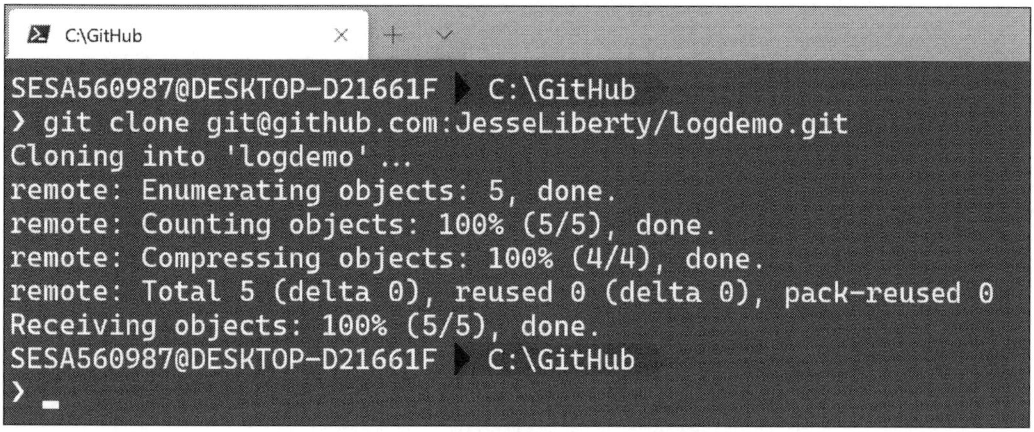

Figure 9.2: Cloning the demo program

With this local repository, we can begin to examine its commits using `log`. To do so, of course, we need to create a program and make some commits.

The LogDemo program

Create a program in the `LogDemo` directory. Change the program to be public and build and run it to make sure it is working:

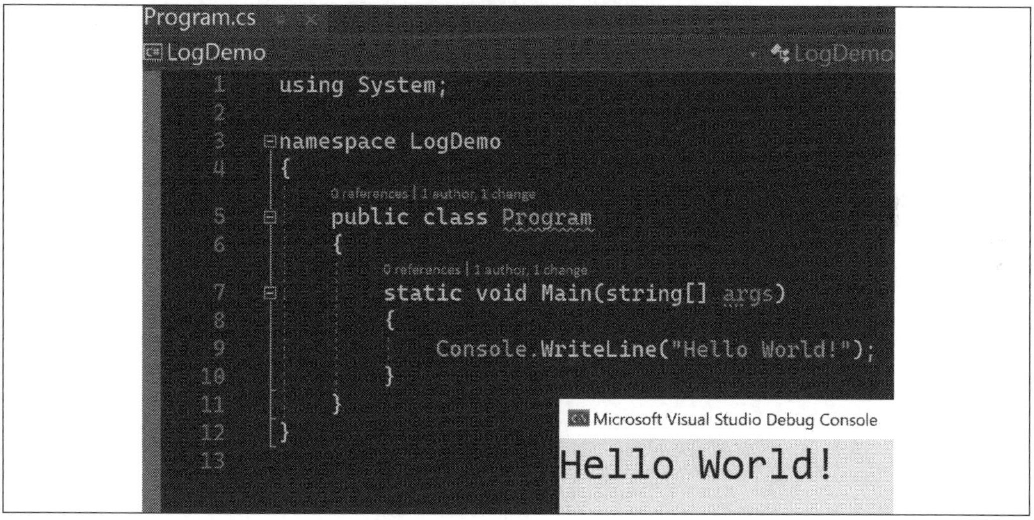

Figure 9.3: Testing the program

I'm going to create the same `calculator` class we've seen before, with the same commits after each tiny function. I'll spare you having to look at all that and I'll just put it into the repository.

Having added all the functions, let's give it a spin:

```
using System;

namespace LogDemo
{
    public class Program
    {
        static void Main(string[] args)
        {
            var calculator = new Calculator.Calculator();
            Console.WriteLine($"5+3 = {calculator.Add(5, 3)}");
            Console.WriteLine($"The square root of 3.14159 is
                {calculator.squareRoot(3.14159)}");
        }
    }
}
```

The results should be:

```
5+3 = 8
The square root of 3.14159 is 1.7724531023414978
```

I now have a number of commits, which we can see using the lg alias described in
Chapter 8, Aliases:

```
> git lg
bec9f25 | Exercise the program [Jesse Liberty] (12 seconds ago) (HEAD → main)
0b09cbe | Call the add function [Jesse Liberty] (12 seconds ago)
8fce349 | Instantiate the calculator [Jesse Liberty] (22 seconds ago)
71c5fb4 | Remove hello world [Jesse Liberty] (10 minutes ago)
f717ed7 | Add square root [Jesse Liberty] (10 minutes ago)
c755be8 | Add division [Jesse Liberty] (11 minutes ago)
c44fcc3 | Add integer division [Jesse Liberty] (12 minutes ago)
094e3d4 | Add the multiply method [Jesse Liberty] (12 minutes ago)
40c287a | Add the subtract method [Jesse Liberty] (13 minutes ago)
16aa1da | Add the add method [Jesse Liberty] (14 minutes ago)
9afca21 | Create calculator class [Jesse Liberty] (17 hours ago)
8798eac | Initial commit [Jesse Liberty] (17 hours ago)
e040fb0 | Initial commit [Jesse Liberty] (17 hours ago) (origin/main, origin/HEAD)
SESA560987@DESKTOP-D21661F ▶ C:\GitHub\logdemo    main ↑12
```

Figure 9.4: Examining the commits with the lg alias of log

We can see that there are 12 commits, and we can see on the last line that none
of them has been pushed, and so we are ahead of origin by 12 commits. That is
confirmed by the status command:

```
> git st
On branch main
Your branch is ahead of 'origin/main' by 12 commits.
  (use "git push" to publish your local commits)

nothing to commit, working tree clean
SESA560987@DESKTOP-D21661F ▶ C:\GitHub\logdemo    main ↑12
>
```

Figure 9.5: Status shows 12 commits to push and nothing in the working directory

Once the commits are made, the working directory is clean. You do have 12 commits ready to be pushed, but that does not affect Git's analysis of the state of the working directory.

Visual Studio

Another great view of this same information is in Visual Studio. Click on **Git**:

Figure 9.6: Click on the menu item Git

And then on **View Branch History**:

Outgoing (12) Push				
bec9f25b	Jesse Liberty	3/1/2021 8:39:07 AM	Exercise the program
0b09cbed	Jesse Liberty	3/1/2021 8:34:02 AM	Call the add function
8fce3491	Jesse Liberty	3/1/2021 8:32:03 AM	Instantiate the calculator
71c5fb4d	Jesse Liberty	3/1/2021 8:30:57 AM	Remove hello world
f717ed7b	Jesse Liberty	3/1/2021 8:30:19 AM	Add square root
c755be83	Jesse Liberty	3/1/2021 8:29:31 AM	Add division
c44fcc3c	Jesse Liberty	3/1/2021 8:28:53 AM	Add integer division
094e3d40	Jesse Liberty	3/1/2021 8:28:18 AM	Add the multiply method
40c287aa	Jesse Liberty	3/1/2021 8:27:46 AM	Add the subtract method
16aa1da1	Jesse Liberty	3/1/2021 8:27:11 AM	Add the add method
9afca210	Jesse Liberty	2/28/2021 3:47:00 PM	Create calculator class
8798eac2	Jesse Liberty	2/28/2021 3:43:43 PM	Initial commit
Local History				
e040fb00	Jesse Liberty	2/28/2021 3:41:34 PM	Initial commit

Figure 9.7: Branch history

This shows the 12 commits ready to be pushed, and the one commit that is already on origin (e040fb00).

GitHub Desktop

GitHub Desktop has yet another way of presenting the same data. This single page tells you a lot in one view:

Figure 9.8: GitHub Desktop

Along the top, we see the repository, branch, and status. Running down the left column are each of the commits and their messages. (Clicking on the up arrow will push that commit.) The middle column shows which files are in that commit, and the far right shows the code from the selected file. The log command can do all of these things, but not all at once.

log at the command line

There are a large number of flags you can add to log to control its output. In creating the lg alias, we already saw how to use log --oneline:

```
> git log --oneline
bec9f25 (HEAD -> main) Exercise the program
0b09cbe Call the add function
8fce349 Instantiate the calculator
71c5fb4 Remove hello world
f717ed7 Add square root
c755be8 Add division
c44fcc3 Add integer division
094e3d4 Add the multiply method
40c287a Add the subtract method
16aa1da Add the add method
9afca21 Create calculator class
8798eac Initial commit
e040fb0 (origin/main, origin/HEAD) Initial commit
```

Figure 9.9: Using log at the command line

Looking closely, we see that the left column has the short ID, the right column lists the messages associated with each commit, and for both the first and last commits, we also see where the head pointer is; both locally and on origin.

Which files changed?

If you want to know which files were changed in each commit but not see what those changes were, you would use:

```
git log --name-only
```

Here is an excerpt:

```
commit 0b09cbedb60fdc23aaee5043df0ac0e33f73718b
Author: Jesse Liberty <JesseLiberty@non.se.com>
Date:   Mon Mar 1 08:34:02 2021 -0500

    Call the add function

LogDemo/LogDemo/Program.cs

commit 8fce349163962f4022ac0b1ea7e8761006f95447
Author: Jesse Liberty <JesseLiberty@non.se.com>
Date:   Mon Mar 1 08:32:03 2021 -0500

    Instantiate the calculator

LogDemo/LogDemo/Program.cs
```

Figure 9.10: Using log to see file changes

We see two commits. The first, in `Program.cs`, has the message `Call the add function`, and you can also see the full ID, the author, and when this commit was made.

You can of course do the same thing with our lg alias to condense the output:

```
8fce349  | Instantiate the calculator [Jesse Liberty]  (23 minutes ago)

LogDemo/LogDemo/Program.cs
71c5fb4  | Remove hello world [Jesse Liberty]  (33 minutes ago)

LogDemo/LogDemo/Program.cs
f717ed7  | Add square root [Jesse Liberty]  (33 minutes ago)

LogDemo/LogDemo/Calculator/Calculator.cs
```

Figure 9.11: Using the shortcut lg

The problem here is that the vertical spacing can be confusing. This example shows three commits. The first has the message Instantiate the calculator and in that commit Program.cs was modified. The best way to figure out which file goes with which commit is to start with the ID.

There is not an easy way to do this in Visual Studio and, as we saw, GitHub Desktop shows you the list of changed files as part of the commit history.

What changed in each file?

We can go further and ask log which files changed and what the files were in that change. The command for this is git log -p.

This will print out the changes for each file in each commit. Here is one file's changes:

```
commit bec9f25b77d4c02a57d33e074724f9e87f43e73c (HEAD → main)
Author: Jesse Liberty <JesseLiberty@non.se.com>
Date:   Mon Mar 1 08:39:07 2021 -0500

    Exercise the program

diff --git a/LogDemo/LogDemo/Program.cs b/LogDemo/LogDemo/Program.cs
index 3de7fa7..2ed69be 100644
--- a/LogDemo/LogDemo/Program.cs
+++ b/LogDemo/LogDemo/Program.cs
@@ -8,6 +8,7 @@ namespace LogDemo
         {
             var calculator = new Calculator.Calculator();
             Console.WriteLine($"5+3 = {calculator.Add(5, 3)}");
+            Console.WriteLine($"The square root of 3.14159 is {calculator.squareRoot(3.14159)}");
         }
     }
}
```

Figure 9.12: Using log to see what has changed in each file

On my computer, the new line is shown in green, and notice the + sign to the left indicating that this line was added. Let's go into `Program.cs` and make some more changes – taking out the square root function and adding a call to the divide function:

```
commit 468d37909bb0ac61bef8ec57fbfe627b47ea4cc8 (HEAD -> main)
Author: Jesse Liberty <JesseLiberty@non.se.com>
Date:   Mon Mar 1 09:15:49 2021 -0500

    Remove square root from test, add divide

diff --git a/LogDemo/LogDemo/Program.cs b/LogDemo/LogDemo/Program.cs
index 2ed69be..110b967 100644
--- a/LogDemo/LogDemo/Program.cs
+++ b/LogDemo/LogDemo/Program.cs
@@ -8,7 +8,7 @@ namespace LogDemo
         {
             var calculator = new Calculator.Calculator();
             Console.WriteLine($"5+3 = {calculator.Add(5, 3)}");
             Console.WriteLine($"The square root of 3.14159 is {calculator.squareRoot(3.14159)}");
+            Console.WriteLine($"5/3 = {calculator.Divide(5/3)}");
         }
     }
 }
```

Figure 9.13: Using diff indicators to see changes

Here `log` is showing that the square root method was removed (red on my screen with a minus sign on the far left) and the divide method was added (once again, note the + sign on the far left).

Just below the message for this commit we see an interesting line:

```
diff --git a/LogDemo/LogDemo/Program.cs b/LogDemo/LogDemo/Program.cs
```

Git is using the `diff` command, separating the original version (a/LogDemo/LogDemo/Program.cs) from the new version (b/LogDemo/LogDemo/Program.cs). It is this use of `diff` that allows log to show the changes.

diff

Nothing stops you from using diff yourself. The most powerful use of this is to show you what has changed in the work you have done since the last commit. You do this before you commit your changes.

Suppose you are doing work and then you are called away. If you are like me, you have completely forgotten how far you've gotten and what exactly you were about to do. Let's add back the square root method and remove the divide method to test the program, but before we commit it, let's see the change:

```
> git diff
diff --git a/LogDemo/LogDemo/Program.cs b/LogDemo/LogDemo/Program.cs
index 110b967..8e26107 100644
--- a/LogDemo/LogDemo/Program.cs
+++ b/LogDemo/LogDemo/Program.cs
@@ -8,7 +8,7 @@ namespace LogDemo
         {
             var calculator = new Calculator.Calculator();
             Console.WriteLine($"5+3 = {calculator.Add(5, 3)}");
             Console.WriteLine($"5/3 = {calculator.Divide(5/3)}");
+            Console.WriteLine($"The square root of 5 = {calculator.squareRoot(5.0)}");
         }
     }
}
SESA560987@DESKTOP-D21661F   C:\GitHub\logdemo   ⚡ main ↑13 +0 ~1 -0 !
```

Figure 9.14: Using diff

This is very similar to the previous example, except that this shows the difference between what I have in my working directory and what was in the previous commit. I can tell that this is a change in my working directory by the ~1 in the prompt – indicating that one file has been modified but not yet checked in.

Visual Studio

Suppose I'm working on my program and I add an Absolute method to the calculator:

```
public double Absolute (double x)
{
    return Math.Abs(x);
}
```

I save that and go off to work on other parts of the program. When I return to the calculator, I know I've made a change but I can't remember what. In Visual Studio, right-click on Calculator.cs and select:

```
git compare with unmodified
```

Visual Studio opens side-by-side windows showing what you've changed in this file since the last commit:

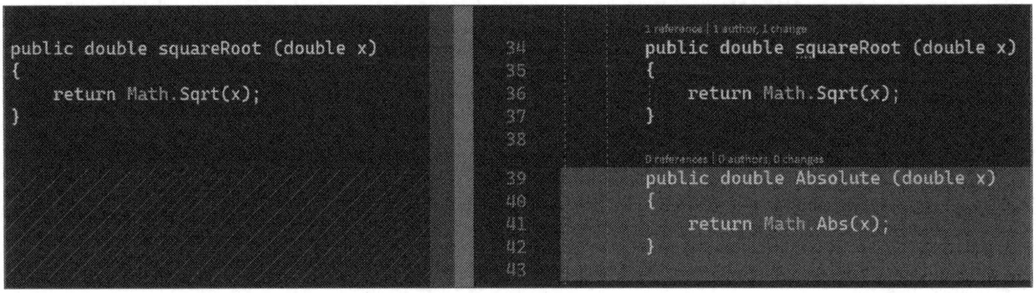

Figure 9.15: Side-by-side comparison

This makes your changes immediately obvious.

What changed in this file over time?

If you want to see the history of changes for a given file, enter:

```
git log <filename>
```

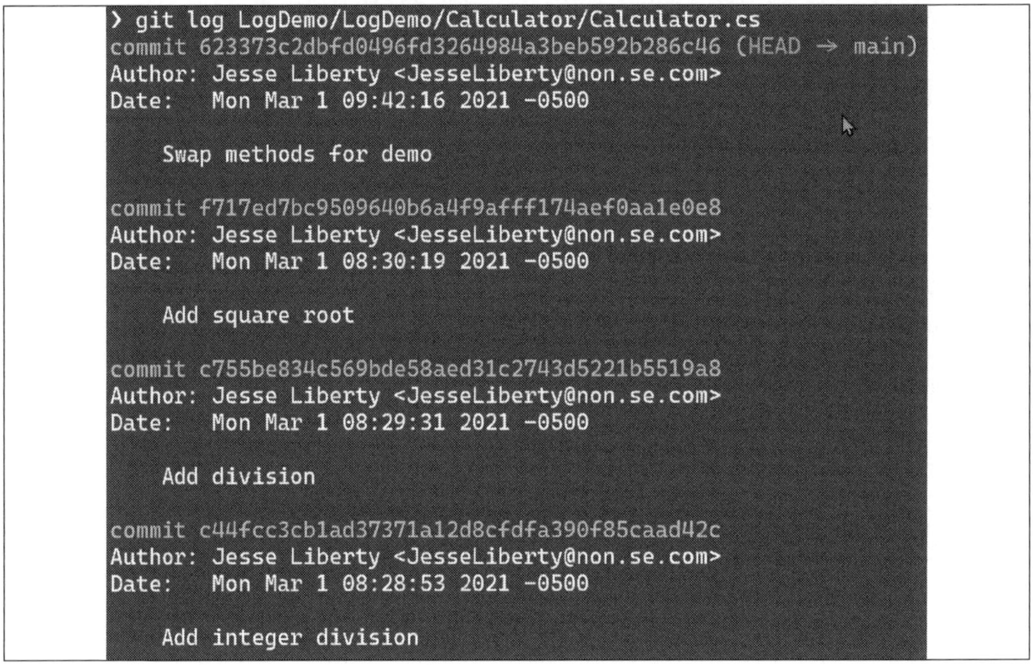

Figure 9.16: Examining changes to one file over time

Here I've asked for a log of `Calculator.cs` (providing the full path) and I get back each change in that file over time. As you might expect, I can make this easier to read with `lg`:

```
> git lg LogDemo/LogDemo/Calculator/Calculator.cs
623373c  | Swap methods for demo [Jesse Liberty] (7 minutes ago) (HEAD → main)
f717ed7  | Add square root [Jesse Liberty] (79 minutes ago)
c755be8  | Add division [Jesse Liberty] (80 minutes ago)
c44fcc3  | Add integer division [Jesse Liberty] (81 minutes ago)
094e3d4  | Add the multiply method [Jesse Liberty] (81 minutes ago)
40c287a  | Add the subtract method [Jesse Liberty] (82 minutes ago)
16aa1da  | Add the add method [Jesse Liberty] (82 minutes ago)
9afca21  | Create calculator class [Jesse Liberty] (18 hours ago)
SESA560987@DESKTOP-D21661F ▶ C:\GitHub\logdemo    ⌥ main ↑14
```

Figure 9.17: Using lg to see what has changed over time

Now we can see what is really going on. The log is providing all the information it usually does, but only for the selected file. Note that the prompt still says we have 14 files to upload, a good hint that this list is not the entire list of commits waiting to be pushed.

Search

Suppose for a moment that we want to find every file in our set of commits that has the word calculator in it. For that we use the `-S` search flag, followed immediately by the term we are searching for:

```
git log -Scalculator
```

This will return all the commits that have the word calculator in one or more of its files:

```
> git log -Scalculator
commit bec9f25b77d4c02a57d33e074724f9e87f43e73c
Author: Jesse Liberty <JesseLiberty@non.se.com>
Date:   Mon Mar 1 08:39:07 2021 -0500

    Exercise the program

commit 0b09cbedb60fdc23aaee5043df0ac0e33f73718b
Author: Jesse Liberty <JesseLiberty@non.se.com>
Date:   Mon Mar 1 08:34:02 2021 -0500

    Call the add function

commit 8fce349163962f4022ac0b1ea7e8761006f95447
Author: Jesse Liberty <JesseLiberty@non.se.com>
Date:   Mon Mar 1 08:32:03 2021 -0500

    Instantiate the calculator
```

Figure 9.18: Searching within commits

Note: You can also use git log -Gcalculator, which will allow you to search on regular expressions.

Once again, the lg alias can make this easier to read:

```
> git lg -Scalculator
bec9f25  | Exercise the program [Jesse Liberty]  (76 minutes ago)
0b09cbe  | Call the add function [Jesse Liberty]  (76 minutes ago)
8fce349  | Instantiate the calculator [Jesse Liberty]  (76 minutes ago)
```

Figure 9.19: Using lg with search

Searching is uncommon, but when you need it, Git provides a very powerful tool.

Where are my commits?

Sometimes you just want the list of commits a particular person has added. To do that, you use:

```
git lg --committer="Jesse"
```

Of course, for this example, that will be all of the commits:

```
> git lg --committer="Jesse Liberty"
623373c  | Swap methods for demo [Jesse Liberty]  (21 minutes ago)  (HEAD → main)
468d379  | Remove square root from test, add divide [Jesse Liberty]  (48 minutes ago)
bec9f25  | Exercise the program [Jesse Liberty]  (83 minutes ago)
0b09cbe  | Call the add function [Jesse Liberty]  (83 minutes ago)
8fce349  | Instantiate the calculator [Jesse Liberty]  (83 minutes ago)
71c5fb4  | Remove hello world [Jesse Liberty]  (2 hours ago)
f717ed7  | Add square root [Jesse Liberty]  (2 hours ago)
c755be8  | Add division [Jesse Liberty]  (2 hours ago)
c44fcc3  | Add integer division [Jesse Liberty]  (2 hours ago)
094e3d4  | Add the multiply method [Jesse Liberty]  (2 hours ago)
40c287a  | Add the subtract method [Jesse Liberty]  (2 hours ago)
16aa1da  | Add the add method [Jesse Liberty]  (2 hours ago)
9afca21  | Create calculator class [Jesse Liberty]  (18 hours ago)
8798eac  | Initial commit [Jesse Liberty]  (18 hours ago)
```

Figure 9.20: Using lg to see what has changed over time

Note that the search is case sensitive, so searching for "jesse liberty" won't return any records, but "Jesse" will.

You may find in practice that you are more interested in the author than who made the commit, and that works the same way, except for using --author.

It turns out, however, that all I want is "Jesse Liberty's" commits in the past 80 minutes. For that we use the since flag (you can put in any reasonable designation of elapsed time, for example, --since="one week"):

```
git lg --since="80 minutes"
```

That produces a much more manageable list:

```
> git lg --committer="Jesse" --since="80 minutes"
623373c | Swap methods for demo [Jesse Liberty] (18 minutes ago) (HEAD → main)
468d379 | Remove square root from test, add divide [Jesse Liberty] (44 minutes ago)
bec9f25 | Exercise the program [Jesse Liberty] (80 minutes ago)
0b09cbe | Call the add function [Jesse Liberty] (80 minutes ago)
8fce349 | Instantiate the calculator [Jesse Liberty] (80 minutes ago)
```

Figure 9.21: Limiting the output of log by time

You can do exactly the same search for author, in case they are not the same:

```
> git lg --author="Jesse" --since="2 hours"
623373c | Swap methods for demo [Jesse Liberty] (29 minutes ago) (HEAD → main)
468d379 | Remove square root from test, add divide [Jesse Liberty] (56 minutes ago)
bec9f25 | Exercise the program [Jesse Liberty] (2 hours ago)
0b09cbe | Call the add function [Jesse Liberty] (2 hours ago)
8fce349 | Instantiate the calculator [Jesse Liberty] (2 hours ago)
71c5fb4 | Remove hello world [Jesse Liberty] (2 hours ago)
f717ed7 | Add square root [Jesse Liberty] (2 hours ago)
c755be8 | Add division [Jesse Liberty] (2 hours ago)
c44fcc3 | Add integer division [Jesse Liberty] (2 hours ago)
094e3d4 | Add the multiply method [Jesse Liberty] (2 hours ago)
40c287a | Add the subtract method [Jesse Liberty] (2 hours ago)
16aa1da | Add the add method [Jesse Liberty] (2 hours ago)
```

Figure 9.22: Limiting the log based on author and time

Limiting the log to a specific time can greatly facilitate zeroing in on the changes you are interested in.

Summary

In this section you've seen the powerful Git command `log` in use. Among the flags we covered were:

log flag	Meaning
`--oneline`	Show only one line per commit
`--name-only`	Names of files that have changed in each commit
`-p`	What has changed?
`git log <filename>`	What has changed in this file?
`-Sfoo`	Search for foo in every commit
`--committer="name"`	Search for all commits by name
`--author="name"`	Search for all authors by name
`--since="1 week"`	Use with committer or author to search within a designated amount of time

Good working knowledge of the most important `log` commands can make working with your commits much easier. Of course, there are many more commands and flags, but it is easy to google the ones you want.

Challenge

In this challenge you will use `log` to examine a set of commits:

1. Create a new repository
2. Create a program in that repository
3. Add a number of (at least 6) commits
4. Find the names of every file changed in each commit
5. Find what changed in a given file over time
6. Find all the files you committed in the past hour (or whatever time increment makes sense)

Notice that you will be using `log` to see how one file changes over time and to find the names of every file in the commit. This shows the versatility of the `log` command.

Answer

There is no one correct answer to this challenge, but unlike some of the other challenges, you are somewhat constrained by how `log` is typically used.

Create a new repository

I will go to GitHub.com and create the `LogChallenge` repository:

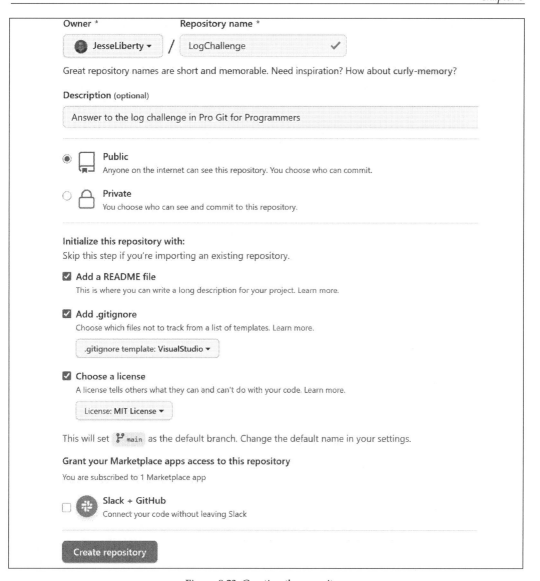

Figure 9.23: Creating the repository

Next, I need to clone that repo to my local machine:

```
git clone git@github.com:JesseLiberty/LogChallenge.git
```

Add at least 6 commits

First, we must track the new program:

```
Untracked files:
  (use "git add <file>..." to include in what will be committed)
        LogChallenge/

nothing added to commit but untracked files present (use "git add" to track)
SESA560987@DESKTOP-D21661F ▶ C:\GitHub\LogChallenge  ⟩ ♭ main ≡ +1 ~0 -0 !
⟩ git add .
SESA560987@DESKTOP-D21661F ▶ C:\GitHub\LogChallenge  ⟩ ♭ main ≡ +3 ~0 -0 ~
⟩
```

Figure 9.24: Tracking the program

We'll add one change to Program.cs:

```
namespace LogChallenge
{
    class Program
    {
        static void Main(string[] args)
        {
            Console.WriteLine("Hello World!");
            Console.WriteLine("Log Challenge!");
        }
    }
}
```

Now it is time to commit that change. Let's start with a call to status (st):

```
⟩ git st
On branch main
Your branch is up to date with 'origin/main'.

Changes to be committed:
  (use "git restore --staged <file>..." to unstage)
        new file:   LogChallenge/LogChallenge.sln
        new file:   LogChallenge/LogChallenge/LogChallenge.csproj
        new file:   LogChallenge/LogChallenge/Program.cs

Changes not staged for commit:
  (use "git add <file>..." to update what will be committed)
  (use "git restore <file>..." to discard changes in working directory)
        modified:   LogChallenge/LogChallenge/Program.cs
```

Figure 9.25: Handling untracked and modified files

This is a tricky image. Make sure you understand why the first three are "to be committed" and the last is not staged for commit. (Hint: the first three are already in the staging area.)

To make life easy, we'll add the unstaged files all at once:

```
> git add .
SESA560987@DESKTOP-D21661F ▶ C:\GitHub\LogChallenge ⟩ ⑂ main ≡ +3 ~0 -0 ~
> git st
On branch main
Your branch is up to date with 'origin/main'.

Changes to be committed:
  (use "git restore --staged <file> ... " to unstage)
        new file:   LogChallenge/LogChallenge.sln
        new file:   LogChallenge/LogChallenge/LogChallenge.csproj
        new file:   LogChallenge/LogChallenge/Program.cs
```

Figure 9.26: Adding the unstaged files

Now make sure you understand why there are three files to be committed and not four (hint: take a look at `Program.cs`).

Go ahead and commit these files:

```
> git cam "First commit"
[main 29cfe55] First commit
 3 files changed, 46 insertions(+)
 create mode 100644 LogChallenge/LogChallenge.sln
 create mode 100644 LogChallenge/LogChallenge/LogChallenge.csproj
 create mode 100644 LogChallenge/LogChallenge/Program.cs
SESA560987@DESKTOP-D21661F ▶ C:\GitHub\LogChallenge ⟩ ⑂ main ↑1
```

Figure 9.27: Making the commits

Once again, I'm using the alias from the previous chapter. Notice that cam adds, but there is nothing to add. No harm done. It then commits and waits for a message. *Do not push the commit at this time.*

Let's add some more commits by creating the `Calculator` class and each method and committing after each change, as you've seen before.

Finally, let's test the `SquareRoot` function in `Program.cs`:

```
namespace LogChallenge
{
    public static class Program
    {
        public static void Main(string[] args)
        {
```

```csharp
            var calculator = new Calculator.Calculator();
            Console.WriteLine($"The square root of 2 is
              {calculator.SquareRoot(2)}");


        }
    }
}
namespace LogChallenge.Calculator
{
    public class Calculator
    {
        public int Add(int left, int right)
        {
            return left + right;
        }
        public int Subtract(int left, int right)
        {
            return left - right;
        }
        public int Multiply(int left, int right)
        {
            return left * right;
        }
        public int IntDivision(int left, int right)
        {
            return left / right;
        }

        public double Division(double left, double right)
        {
            return left / right;
        }

        public int Modulus(int left, int right)
        {
```

```
        return left % right;
    }
    public double SquareRoot(double x)
    {
        return Math.Sqrt(x);
    }


    }
}
```

Running this gives the correct result as a double:

```
The square root of 2 is 1.4142135623730951
```

Let's examine the messages of all the commits:

```
> git lg
43dd70e  | test the square root function [Jesse Liberty]  (5 minutes
ago)  (HEAD -> main)
0fa51fa  | make Main public and remove writelines [Jesse Liberty]  (8
minutes ago)
51dd6e9  | Add square root function [Jesse Liberty]  (8 minutes ago)
711c4e8  | add modulus operator [Jesse Liberty]  (9 minutes ago)
06d7319  | add division function [Jesse Liberty]  (10 minutes ago)
31f5873  | Add intDivision function [Jesse Liberty]  (11 minutes ago)
9639a70  | add the multiply function [Jesse Liberty]  (12 minutes ago)
d1eaff5  | capitalize subtract function [Jesse Liberty]  (12 minutes
ago)
d92657d  | Add subtract function [Jesse Liberty]  (13 minutes ago)
b5e945f  | Capitalize add function [Jesse Liberty]  (13 minutes ago)
f535d26  | Add the add function [Jesse Liberty]  (14 minutes ago)
a8cf101  | make calculator class public [Jesse Liberty]  (15 minutes
ago)
acd2ce4  | Create calculator class [Jesse Liberty]  (15 minutes ago)
29cfe55  | First commit [Jesse Liberty]  (19 minutes ago)
d0518a1  | Initial commit [Jesse Liberty]  (41 minutes ago)  (origin/
main, origin/HEAD)
```

There is a bit of extra information here (the ID, the author, and so on.) but we do see the messages of all the commits:

```
> git lg --name-only
43dd70e   | test the square root function [Jesse Liberty]  (8 minutes ago)  (HEAD → main)

LogChallenge/LogChallenge/Program.cs
0fa51fa   | make Main public and remove writelines [Jesse Liberty]  (11 minutes ago)

LogChallenge/LogChallenge/Program.cs
51dd6e9   | Add square root function [Jesse Liberty]  (11 minutes ago)

LogChallenge/LogChallenge/Calculator/Calculator.cs
711c4e8   | add modulus operator [Jesse Liberty]  (12 minutes ago)

LogChallenge/LogChallenge/Calculator/Calculator.cs
06d7319   | add division function [Jesse Liberty]  (13 minutes ago)

LogChallenge/LogChallenge/Calculator/Calculator.cs
31f5873   | Add intDivision function [Jesse Liberty]  (14 minutes ago)

LogChallenge/LogChallenge/Calculator/Calculator.cs
9639a70   | add the multiply function [Jesse Liberty]  (15 minutes ago)

LogChallenge/LogChallenge/Calculator/Calculator.cs
d1eaff5   | capitalize subtract function [Jesse Liberty]  (15 minutes ago)
```

Figure 9.28: Using lg with the name only flag

Now that we've seen how to handle staged and unstaged files and examine their contents with log, let's see how to find every file in a commit that actually changed.

Find the names of every file changed in each commit

This is tricky because of the spacing. Let's examine the first one; first, we see the ID and message from the latest commit, and then some way down we see the affected file. Similarly, in the second box, we see **Add square root function**, but the affected file, Calculator.cs, is a bit further down the listing. This is clearer with a couple of files. Let's do that.

We'll add the Round method to Calculator:

```
public decimal Round(decimal x)
{
    return  Math.Round(x);
}
```

And we'll test it in the program:

```csharp
public static void Main(string[] args)
{
    var calculator = new Calculator.Calculator();
    Console.WriteLine($"The square root of 93 is
      {calculator.SquareRoot(93)}");
    Console.WriteLine($"93.64 rounded is " +
        $"{calculator.Round((decimal)93.64)}");
}
```

We now check it in, and we have made changes to two files:

```
modified:   LogChallenge/LogChallenge/Calculator/Calculator.cs
modified:   LogChallenge/LogChallenge/Program.cs
```

Figure 9.29: Seeing that two files are modified

We check that in, and we now have 15 commits:

```
> git lg
d2dfd23 | Make program static, add round to calculator [Jesse Liberty]  (36 seconds ago)  (HEAD → main)
43dd70e | test the square root function [Jesse Liberty]  (5 hours ago)
0fa51fa | make Main public and remove writelines [Jesse Liberty]  (6 hours ago)
51dd6e9 | Add square root function [Jesse Liberty]  (6 hours ago)
711c4e8 | add modulus operator [Jesse Liberty]  (6 hours ago)
06d7319 | add division function [Jesse Liberty]  (6 hours ago)
31f5873 | Add intDivision function [Jesse Liberty]  (6 hours ago)
9639a70 | add the multiply function [Jesse Liberty]  (6 hours ago)
d1eaff5 | capitalize subtract function [Jesse Liberty]  (6 hours ago)
d92657d | Add subtract function [Jesse Liberty]  (6 hours ago)
b5e945f | Capitalize add function [Jesse Liberty]  (6 hours ago)
f535d26 | Add the add function [Jesse Liberty]  (6 hours ago)
a8cf101 | make calculator class public [Jesse Liberty]  (6 hours ago)
acd2ce4 | Create calculator class [Jesse Liberty]  (6 hours ago)
29cfe55 | First commit [Jesse Liberty]  (6 hours ago)
d0518a1 | Initial commit [Jesse Liberty]  (6 hours ago)  (origin/main, origin/HEAD)
SESA560987@DESKTOP-D21661F ▶ C:\GitHub\LogChallenge ⑂ main ↑15
```

Figure 9.30: Using lg to examine the 15 commits

Find what changed in a given file over time

To find what has changed in a file over time, we use the simple `log` command with the name of the file we want to see. For example, we can examine the changes to `Program.cs` (remember to include the relative path):

```
git log LogChallenge/LogChallenge/Program.cs
```

The result shows all the commits, with the latest at the top:

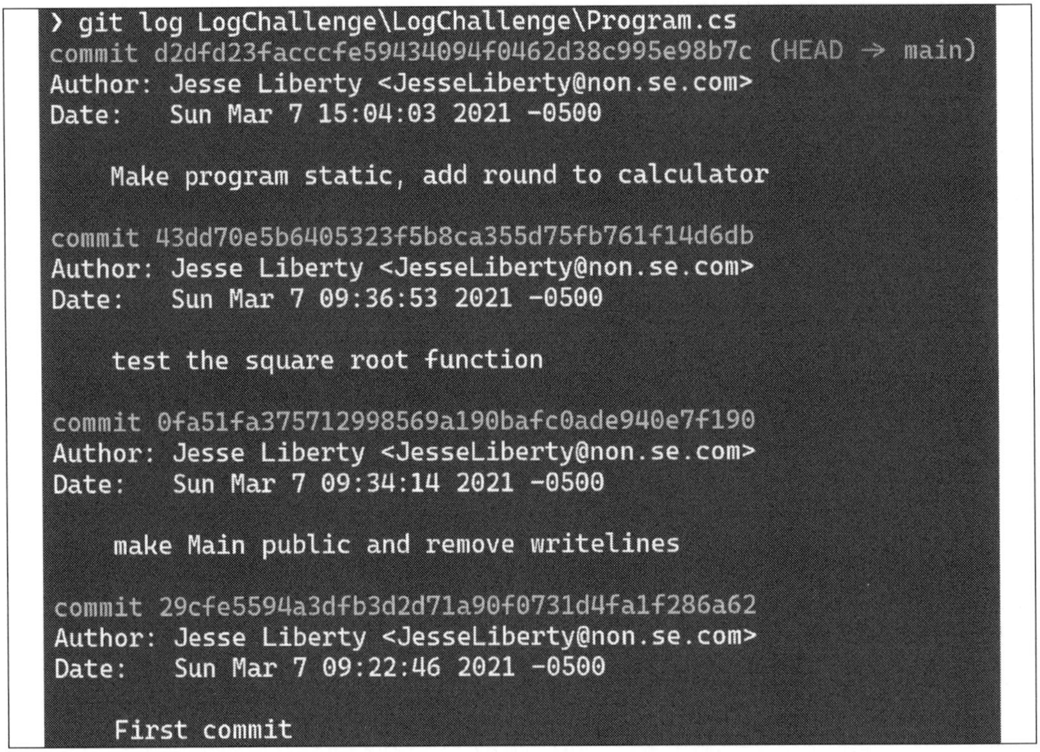

```
> git log LogChallenge\LogChallenge\Program.cs
commit d2dfd23facccfe59434094f0462d38c995e98b7c (HEAD → main)
Author: Jesse Liberty <JesseLiberty@non.se.com>
Date:    Sun Mar 7 15:04:03 2021 -0500

    Make program static, add round to calculator

commit 43dd70e5b6405323f5b8ca355d75fb761f14d6db
Author: Jesse Liberty <JesseLiberty@non.se.com>
Date:    Sun Mar 7 09:36:53 2021 -0500

    test the square root function

commit 0fa51fa375712998569a190bafc0ade940e7f190
Author: Jesse Liberty <JesseLiberty@non.se.com>
Date:    Sun Mar 7 09:34:14 2021 -0500

    make Main public and remove writelines

commit 29cfe5594a3dfb3d2d71a90f0731d4fa1f286a62
Author: Jesse Liberty <JesseLiberty@non.se.com>
Date:    Sun Mar 7 09:22:46 2021 -0500

    First commit
```

Figure 9.31: All the commits for one file

We have seen how to find all the commits for one file over time, but that can be a bit overwhelming. We may want only the most recent commits.

Find all the files you committed in the past hour (or whatever time increment makes sense)

For this, we need only the since flag:

```
> git log --since="90 minutes"
commit d2dfd23facccfe59434094f0462d38c995e98b7c (HEAD → main)
Author: Jesse Liberty <JesseLiberty@non.se.com>
Date:    Sun Mar 7 15:04:03 2021 -0500

    Make program static, add round to calculator
```

Figure 9.32: Using the since flag

We have fulfilled the challenge by doing the following:

- Creating a new repository
- Creating a program in that repository
- Adding commits
- Finding the names of every file changed in each commit
- Examining the changes in one file over time
- Finding all the files committed in the past hour

10
Important Git Commands and Metadata

There are hundreds of Git commands and flags. In this chapter, we'll endeavor to review a few of the most important that we have not looked at so far. These include:

- Creating the stash
- Listing what's in the stash
- Retrieving from the stash
- The clean command for getting rid of unwanted untracked files
- How to see metadata and choose which data you want to see

Let's start by digging into the stash.

You can find the complete list at http://git-scm.com/docs.

Stash

When we reviewed the five areas of Git, we included an area called the stash, but we did not delve into what the stash is. In short, the stash is a place where you can hold (stash) files you've modified but not yet committed:

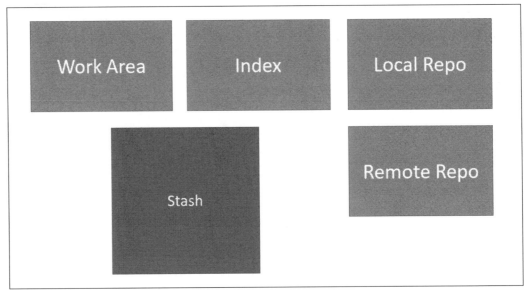

Figure 10.1: The five areas of Git

The stash can be pretty important. Let's say you are working on a feature and suddenly you are asked to work on a very important bug. You are not ready to commit the code you have, but you can't switch branches with uncommitted files in the work area.

To solve this, you *could* just make a backup of your directory, and then delete the uncommitted files, but that is very slow and error-prone. Instead, you want to stash them away somewhere that you can get them back when you are ready, which of course is the purpose of the stash.

To see this at work, we need a repository with some commits. Let's quickly make a mirror of the RockyHorror2 repo. To do so, we'll start by making sure we have the RockyHorror2 repository on disk, or else we'll pull it from the server.

Let's go to GitHub and create a repo called `RockyHorrorStash`:

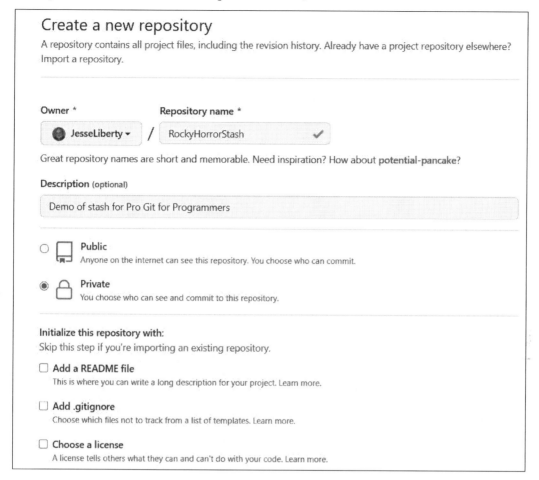

Figure 10.2: Creating the repository

Notice that I did not bother creating a readme, .gitignore, nor a license since these will all be overwritten when I do the mirror.

Click **Create Repository** and once created, grab its address.

We are now ready to mirror `RockyHorror2` over `RockyHorrorStash`. Be sure to change directory to `RockyHorror2` and enter this command:

```
jesse@Win10  ~  source  repos  rockyhorror2    main ≡
> git push --mirror https://github.com/JesseLiberty/RockyHorrorStash.git
Enumerating objects: 42, done.
Counting objects: 100% (42/42), done.
Delta compression using up to 8 threads
Compressing objects: 100% (23/23), done.
Writing objects: 100% (42/42), 7.78 KiB | 419.00 KiB/s, done.
Total 42 (delta 18), reused 39 (delta 18), pack-reused 0
remote: Resolving deltas: 100% (18/18), done.
To https://github.com/JesseLiberty/RockyHorrorStash.git
 * [new branch]      main → main
 * [new reference]   refs/notes/commits → refs/notes/commits
 * [new reference]   origin/HEAD → origin/HEAD
 * [new reference]   origin/main → origin/main
 * [new tag]         LastShowCommit → LastShowCommit
```

Figure 10.3: Push the mirrored repo to the remote

We now have the mirrored repo on the server but not locally, so let's clone it:

```
jesse@Win10  ~  source  repos
> git clone https://github.com/JesseLiberty/RockyHorrorStash.git
Cloning into 'RockyHorrorStash' ...
remote: Enumerating objects: 39, done.
remote: Counting objects: 100% (39/39), done.
remote: Compressing objects: 100% (21/21), done.
remote: Total 39 (delta 18), reused 39 (delta 18), pack-reused 0
Receiving objects: 100% (39/39), 7.53 KiB | 2.51 MiB/s, done.
Resolving deltas: 100% (18/18), done.
```

Figure 10.4: Pull the mirrored repo back to the local repo

Great, we have a repo we can work with. Let's see what's in it with a quick call to log:

```
git lg
e16d191 - (HEAD → main, origin/main, origin/HEAD) Add program.cs first modifications (7 days ago) <Jesse Liberty>
f55eb6e - Instantiate a showing (13 days ago) <Jesse Liberty>
bb4927c - Remove hello world (13 days ago) <Jesse Liberty>
bf6b900 - (tag: LastShowCommit) Enter show times (13 days ago) <Jesse Liberty>
32495b0 - How many seats are there at this location (13 days ago) <Jesse Liberty>
04ceafe - Add location property (13 days ago) <Jesse Liberty>
98b26f9 - Create Showing Class (13 days ago) <Jesse Liberty>
b1dbf7b - Initial creation of program (13 days ago) <Jesse Liberty>
d396657 - Initial commit (13 days ago) <Jesse Liberty>
```

Figure 10.5: Examining the local repo with log

Suppose we are working on this project and we modify two files. First, we modify the Showing class to keep count of how many boxes of popcorn are sold:

```
1 reference | Jesse Liberty, 13 days ago | 1 author, 4 changes
public class Showing
{
        2 references | Jesse Liberty, 13 days ago | 1 author, 1 change
        public string Location { get; set; }
        2 references | Jesse Liberty, 13 days ago | 1 author, 1 change
        public int NumberOfSeats { get; set; }
        2 references | Jesse Liberty, 13 days ago | 1 author, 1 change
        public List<DateTime> ShowTimes { get; set; }

        0 references | 0 changes | 0 authors, 0 changes
        public int PopcornSold { get; set; }
}
```

Figure 10.6: Adding the Showing class

Next, we modify Program.cs to say that the Brattle theater has 500 seats. If we take a status, we see the two modified files in the work area:

```
> git st
On branch main
Your branch is up to date with 'origin/main'.

Changes not staged for commit:
  (use "git add <file>..." to update what will be committed)
  (use "git restore <file>..." to discard changes in working directory)
        modified:   RockyHorror/Program.cs
        modified:   RockyHorror/Showing.cs

no changes added to commit (use "git add" and/or "git commit -a")
```

Figure 10.7: git status shows two modified files

We have two uncommitted modified files. We have more work to do but our boss calls and she tells us that there is an urgent bug in another project. This is where stash comes in. We *could* commit what we have, but we're not ready to, so let's put it in the stash:

```
> git stash
Saved working directory and index state WIP on main: e16d191 Add program.cs first modifications
```

Figure 10.8: Adding to the stash

You tell it `git stash`, and it takes everything in the work area and in the index and puts it in the stash without committing it. At that point, the work area is reset to the state it was in before you started modifying files—that is the previous position of HEAD.

You can see what is in your stash with the `stash list` command:

```
> git stash list
stash@{0}: WIP on main: e16d191 Add program.cs first modifications
```

Figure 10.9: Listing what is in the stash

The stash has added the designation `WIP on main`. WIP means Work In Progress.

At the moment, you only have one thing in the stash. You might find, however, that while fixing that "very important bug," your boss calls back and says to stop work on that and fix a fatal bug. Once again, you may need to stash your work. Rather than setting all that up, we'll make a small change in the main program and then stash it. Let's change the name of the theater:

```
showing.Location = "Limestone";
showing.NumberOfSeats = 250;
```

Figure 10.10: Stashing more work

Hey! What happened to the number of seats being increased to 500? Remember, we never committed that, we stashed it away and the working area was reset. Let's take a look at the status:

```
> git st
On branch main
Your branch is up to date with 'origin/main'.

Changes not staged for commit:
  (use "git add <file> ... " to update what will be committed)
  (use "git restore <file> ... " to discard changes in working directory)
        modified:   RockyHorror/Program.cs

no changes added to commit (use "git add" and/or "git commit -a")
```

Figure 10.11: Examining the status

As we expect, we see the one modification we've made. Let's stash that away using `git stash`:

```
> git stash
Saved working directory and index state WIP on main: e16d191 Add program.cs first modifications
```

Figure 10.12: Stashing the modification

We now have two items in the stash. If we ask for a list, we should see both:

```
> git stash list
stash@{0}: WIP on main: e16d191 Add program.cs first modifications
stash@{1}: WIP on main: e16d191 Add program.cs first modifications
```

Figure 10.13: Listing the items in the stash

Sure enough, both stashed items are there. Normally they would have different ID and messages, but since we stashed from the same place, we ended up with this anomalous situation. You can see what is in the stash by using `stash show`:

```
> git stash show
RockyHorror/Program.cs | 2 +-
1 file changed, 1 insertion(+), 1 deletion(-)
```

Figure 10.14: Showing the contents of the stash

You can drop items from the stash and you can clear the entire stash with `stash clear`.

Clean

From time to time, you'll find that there are untracked files listed in your status. 99% of the time these will be files you created and you'll want them to be tracked, which you do by adding them to the index (as shown previously). There are times, however, when you may find untracked files that you don't want:

```
> git st
On branch main
Your branch is up to date with 'origin/main'.

Untracked files:
  (use "git add <file>..." to include in what will be committed)
        Untracked.cs

nothing added to commit but untracked files present (use "git add" to track)
```

Figure 10.15: Untracked files

In this case, we have a couple choices. We can add `Untracked.cs` to the index or we can get rid of it. To do so, we try `git clean`:

```
> git clean
fatal: clean.requireForce defaults to true and neither -i, -n, nor -f given; refusing to clean
```

Figure 10.16: Using clean to remove untracked files (fails)

Because git clean is one of the few truly destructive commands—once called, the untracked files are gone, never to be seen again—Git comes back with the snarky reply that it is "refusing to clean." To actually clean, Git requires that you tell it you really mean it by using the -f (force) flag:

```
> git clean -f
Removing Untracked.cs
```

Figure 10.17: Using clean as above, but with the force flag (succeeds)

The -f flag essentially says "I know what I'm doing"—so make sure you do.

Metadata

Every commit, merge, and so on, is accompanied by metadata. You can get at a lot of the metadata by using the log, but sometimes you just want to extract a few pieces of important metadata. For that you can use the show command:

```
> git show -s HEAD --format='%an <%ae> %h %d'
Jesse Liberty <jesseliberty@gmail.com> e16d191  (HEAD → main, origin/main, origin/HEAD)
```

Figure 10.18: Using show to see metadata

In this example, we use show to find the name and email of the author, along with the ID and the metadata telling us where the tip of main is. Let's break it down:

- git show—the show command.
- -s—silent (or quiet), which suppresses the difference output (try the command without it to see).
- HEAD tells show which commit you are interested in.
- %an is the author's name.
- %ae is the author's email address.

We put this code into a string and assign it to the format flag.

Let's look at the log and see what else we can do with showing metadata:

```
> git lg
* e16d191 - (HEAD → main, origin/main, origin/HEAD) Add program.cs first modifications (7 days ago) <Jesse Liberty>
* f56eb4e - Instantiate a showing (13 days ago) <Jesse Liberty>
* bb4927c - Remove hello world (13 days ago) <Jesse Liberty>
* bf6b900 - (tag: LastShowCommit) Enter show times (13 days ago) <Jesse Liberty>
* 32495b0 - How many seats are there at this location (13 days ago) <Jesse Liberty>
* 84ceafe - Add location property (13 days ago) <Jesse Liberty>
* 98b26f9 - Create Showing Class (13 days ago) <Jesse Liberty>
* b1dbf7b - Initial creation of program (13 days ago) <Jesse Liberty>
* d396657 - Initial commit (13 days ago) <Jesse Liberty>
```

Figure 10.19: Looking at the log

Let's zero in on the metadata associated with one of these entries. To do so, we use the ID:

```
> git show -s bf6b900 --format='%an <%ae> %h %d'
Jesse Liberty <jesseliberty@gmail.com> bf6b900  (tag: LastShowCommit)
```

Figure 10.20: Using show -s to see metadata

You can also specify a range of entries:

```
> git show -s 32495b0..f55eb4e --format='%an <%ae> %h %d'
Jesse Liberty <jesseliberty@gmail.com> f55eb4e
Jesse Liberty <jesseliberty@gmail.com> bb4927c
Jesse Liberty <jesseliberty@gmail.com> bf6b900  (tag: LastShowCommit)
```

Figure 10.21: Specifying a range of entries

We are able to zero in on what we want in the stash. To retrieve the stashed files, use git stash apply. This will apply everything in the stash to the current working directory. Once you are sure you have what you need, you can then call git stash pop, which will apply the changes again and remove them from the stash.

Summary

In this chapter, we reviewed some of the most important commands that we had not yet looked at. These include:

- Creating the stash
- Listing what's in the stash
- Retrieving from the stash
- The clean command for getting rid of unwanted untracked files
- How to see metadata and choose which data you want to see

Challenge

Mirror a repo, or use one you already have if you don't mind changing it. Examine the list of commits. Start work on some changes but don't commit your changes. Switch to working on a different repo. Create or modify some files in the second repo but don't commit them. Start work on a third repo. Abandon that work and go back to the first repository. Examine the stash and retrieve the stash you need to keep working.

Answer

Once again, there are many ways to answer this. I'll start by mirroring the RockyHorrorStash repo to RockyHorrorStash2, and then I will immediately clone it to my local repo.

I'll do the same thing with Panofy (to PanofyStash) and musicHandler2 (creating musicHandler2Stash). Now we have three repos we can work on:

- musicHandler2Stash
- PanofyStash
- RockyHorrorStash

Let's begin with musicHandler2Stash by changing directory and getting a log of what is already there. Then let's open it in Visual Studio and do some work:

```
> git lg
* be3e502 - (HEAD → main, origin/main, origin/HEAD) Add Ripple (2 weeks ago) <Jesse Liberty>
* aa2824c - Drag music into project (2 weeks ago) <Jesse Liberty>
* 2b20307 - Fix namespace (2 weeks ago) <Jesse Liberty>
* 817b28e - Add music class (2 weeks ago) <Jesse Liberty>
* d27ecd0 - # This is a combination of 3 commits. # This is the 1st commit message: (2 weeks ago) <Jesse Liberty>
* 238230b - Initial Commit (3 weeks ago) <Jesse Liberty>
* b6fc88f - Initial commit (3 weeks ago) <Jesse Liberty>
```

Figure 10.22: Log of MusicHandler2Stash

Let's make two changes by opening Visual Studio in that directory. We need changes in a couple of files, so let's just add comments. When we take a status, we see that there are two modified files:

```
> git st
On branch main
Your branch is up to date with 'origin/main'.

Changes not staged for commit:
  (use "git add <file>..." to update what will be committed)
  (use "git restore <file>..." to discard changes in working directory)
        modified:   MusicHandler/Music.cs
        modified:   MusicHandler/Program.cs
```

Figure 10.23: Status of MusicHandler files after changes and before commit

Right in the middle of our work, we're asked to work on a bug. We're not ready to check in these files so we add them to the stash:

```
> git stash
Saved working directory and index state WIP on main: be3e502 Add Ripple
  jesse@Win10    ~  > source > repos > musicHandler2Stash   main ≡
> git status
On branch main
Your branch is up to date with 'origin/main'.
```

Figure 10.24: Call stash, which puts the modified files into the stash,
then call status to see the working directory is empty

We are now free to change to the RockyHorrorStash directory. Here we will start fixing the bug (which we will do by adding comments to represent the real work). Uh oh, we have to work on a bigger bug. Let's stash the work we did in RockyHorrorStash.

We'll switch to PanofyStash and make some changes and commit them. We are now ready to return to the bug we were working on in musicHandler2stash as that has now become the priority. The first thing to do is to list what we have in the stash for this repository (remember, stashes are per repository):

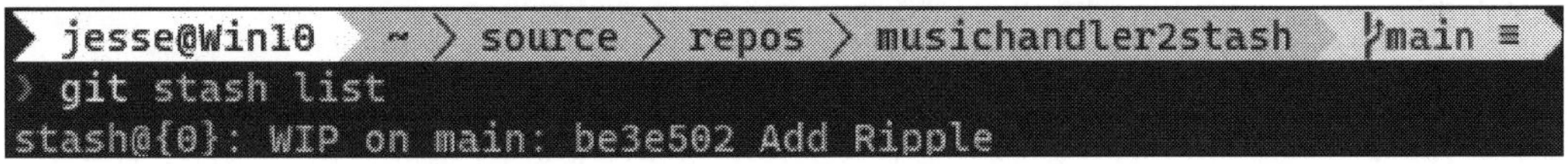

```
  jesse@Win10    ~  > source > repos > musichandler2stash    main ≡
> git stash list
stash@{0}: WIP on main: be3e502 Add Ripple
```

Figure 10.25: stash list in musicHandler2stash

Let's restore that. There are two ways to do so:

- apply applies the stashed files but leaves them in the stash.
- pop applies the stashed files but removes them from the stash.

I recommend using `apply` because it leaves a copy of the stashed items in the:

```
> git stash apply
On branch main
Your branch is up to date with 'origin/main'.

Changes not staged for commit:
  (use "git add <file>..." to update what will be committed)
  (use "git restore <file>..." to discard changes in working directory)
        modified:   MusicHandler/Music.cs
        modified:   MusicHandler/Program.cs

no changes added to commit (use "git add" and/or "git commit -a")
 jesse@Win10    ~  source  repos  musichandler2stash   main ≡ □ ~2
> git st
On branch main
Your branch is up to date with 'origin/main'.

Changes not staged for commit:
  (use "git add <file>..." to update what will be committed)
  (use "git restore <file>..." to discard changes in working directory)
        modified:   MusicHandler/Music.cs
        modified:   MusicHandler/Program.cs
```

Figure 10.26: stash apply

In *Figure 10.26* we first call `git stash apply`. Be very careful with this — there is a different command, `git apply`, which is not what you want here.

Once applied you can see that the two files that were modified are back. We take a status to make sure everything is as we expect. Now that we know it is safe, we can clean out the stash:

```
> git stash list
stash@{0}: WIP on main: be3e502 Add Ripple
 jesse@Win10    ~  source  repos  musichandler2stash   main ≡ □ ~2
> git stash drop
Dropped refs/stash@{0} (7284ecdd5324323692f9e4b0cb9bd114fd7ece44)
 jesse@Win10    ~  source  repos  musichandler2stash   main ≡ □ ~2
> git stash list
 jesse@Win10    ~  source  repos  musichandler2stash   main ≡ □ ~2
```

Figure 10.27: Dropping the cache

In *Figure 10.27* we list what's in the stash, then we drop the stash, and then list again to make sure it is gone.

In this challenge, we mirrored three repos so that we could work on them without changing their original state. We then looked at what commits were there and added new files without committing them. In order to be able to switch repositories, we stashed the uncommitted files. When we returned to the original project, we were able to retrieve the stashed items.

11
Finding a Broken Commit: Bisect and Blame

Sooner or later, you are likely to find that you have a bug in your program that was introduced sometime in the past. You can go searching through all your prior commits, but that is time consuming and inefficient. Git provides a command, bisect, to take care of all the hard work for you.

Here's how it works: bisect asks you for a known "bad" commit. Most often this is the last commit. It then asks for a known "good" commit – that is, a commit that is known to work. You do not have to try out a variety of commits to find this; just far back enough that you can be sure it was working back then.

If you are cautious, you may want to check out the good commit and run it just to make sure.

Bisect will then do a series of binary searches looking to find the first bad commit. If you have good unit tests, bisect can do this on its own; otherwise you must test each commit it finds and report whether it is good or bad.

You begin by entering `git bisect start`. This enters the bisect state, not unlike the way we might enter the rebase state.

Your second command is to tell bisect that the current commit is broken (not working, or in bisect's terminology, *bad*). You indicate this by entering `git bisect bad`.

You now need to tell bisect a good checkout. You can do this in one of two ways: either give it the ID of a good commit, or tell it how many commits to go back from the current, for example `git checkout HEAD~12`, indicating that we know that things were working twelve commits ago.

Git will divide the remaining commits roughly in half, and check out a commit. Let's say that this is the commit made six commits prior to the current one. You then test that commit and tell bisect if it is good or bad.

If you say it is good, that means that every commit before it is good. If you say it is bad, that means that every commit after it is bad. Let's assume commit 6 is good. Bisect will now consider its range to be 6 to 12 and might check out commit 9.

You test commit 9 and find that it is bad. That means that every commit after 9 is bad. Bisect now has a range of 6 to 9 and checks out 7. If 7 is good then the bad commit is either 8 or 9. We test 8 and get the answer: if it is good then 9 is the first bad commit, otherwise it is 8.

All of this is much easier to see with an example. Let's create a new repository called `BisectTest`:

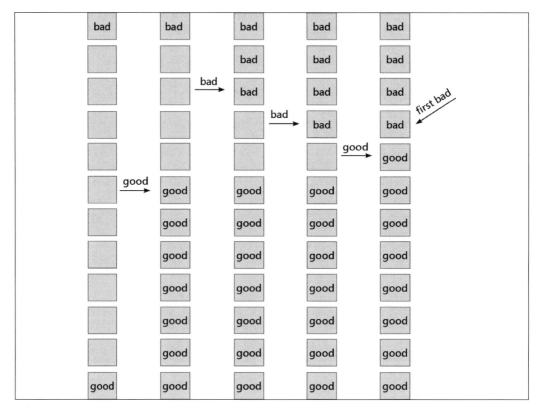

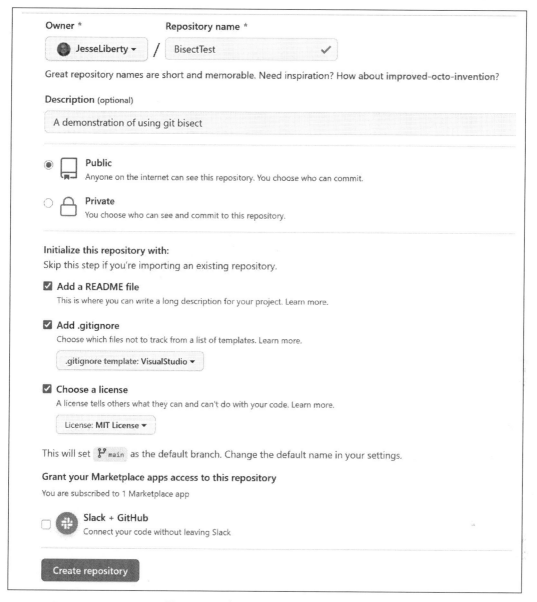

Figure 11.1: The repo to demonstrate bisect

Now, clone that repository to your local disk as we've done before. To demonstrate how this works, we're going to create 12 commits, with one in the middle that has an error that will propagate until someone notices that the program is broken after checking in commit 12. "Oh no," we can hear that programmer cry, "this could have been broken for a long time, with no one noticing. I need to use bisect to find out which commit was bad and fix it."

Let's use our tried-and-true `Calculator` class to create 12 commits. The first will just create the project:

```
using System;

namespace BisectTest
{
    0 references | 0 authors, 0 changes
    public static class Program
    {
        0 references | 0 authors, 0 changes
        static void Main(string[] args)
        {
            Console.WriteLine("Hello World!");
        }
    }
}
```

Figure 11.2: The beginning of our program

We'll save and commit that as our first commit:

```
> git st
On branch main
Your branch is up to date with 'origin/main'.

Untracked files:
  (use "git add <file> ..." to include in what will be committed)
        BisectTest/

nothing added to commit but untracked files present (use "git add" to track)
SESA560987@DESKTOP-D21661F   C:\GitHub\BisectTest    main ≡ +1 ~0 -0 !
> git add .
SESA560987@DESKTOP-D21661F   C:\GitHub\BisectTest    main ≡ +3 ~0 -0 ~
> git commit
[main 174a008] Create the project
 3 files changed, 45 insertions(+)
 create mode 100644 BisectTest/BisectTest.sln
 create mode 100644 BisectTest/BisectTest/BisectTest.csproj
 create mode 100644 BisectTest/BisectTest/Program.cs
SESA560987@DESKTOP-D21661F   C:\GitHub\BisectTest    main ↑1
> git lg
174a008  | Create the project [Jesse Liberty] (26 seconds ago)  (HEAD → main)
7259bb3  | Initial commit [Jesse Liberty] (8 minutes ago)  (origin/main, origin/HEAD)
SESA560987@DESKTOP-D21661F   C:\GitHub\BisectTest    main ↑1
```

Figure 11.3: Save and commit

Next we'll create the `Calculator` class and commit that:

```
namespace BisectTest
{
    public class Calculator
    {
    }
}
```

That makes three commits: the initial commit created when you cloned it, the commit after creating the program, and this commit after creating the `Calculator` class:

```
> git lg
e7e308c  | Add calculator class [Jesse Liberty]  (18 seconds ago)  (HEAD -> main)
174a008  | Create the project [Jesse Liberty]  (5 minutes ago)
7259bb3  | Initial commit [Jesse Liberty]  (12 minutes ago)  (origin/main, origin/HEAD)
```

Figure 11.4: The three commits

Now we'll add the four functions (add, subtract, multiply, and integer division) and commit after each one. After doing so, we have seven commits.

Let's add the modulus operator, real division, and square root, committing after each one.

That gives us ten commits. Next, we'll go back to the program and use the calculator to print out the value of 23/4 using integer division, which gives us the value 5. Let's check that in.

Next, we'll use the modulus operator on the same division:

```
namespace BisectTest
{
    public static class Program
    {
        static void Main(string[] args)
        {
            var calculator = new Calculator();
            Console.WriteLine($"Integer division of 23/4 is
              {calculator.Divide(23, 4)}");
            Console.WriteLine(
                $"Modulus 23%4 is {calculator.Modulus(23, 4)}");
        }
    }
}
```

Finally, we'll divide using doubles:

```
using System;

namespace BisectTest
{
    public static class Program
    {
        static void Main(string[] args)
        {
            var calculator = new Calculator();
            Console.WriteLine($"Integer division of 23/4 is
                {calculator.Divide(23, 4)}");
            Console.WriteLine($"Modulus 23%4 is
                {calculator.Modulus(23, 4)}");
            Console.WriteLine($"Real division of 23/4 is
                {calculator.Divide(23.0, 4.0)}");


        }
    }
}
```

Okay, we're ready to show off our results at the next code review. We run the program and we get:

```
Integer division of 23/4 is 5
Modulus 23%4 is 5
Real division of 23/4 is 5.75
```

That result can't be right. Now, in this case, the problem is obvious; our modulus operator is off. But in the real world, the answer will be far less obvious, let alone where it was introduced.

Let's use bisect to find the commit where we went wrong. We start up bisect, and then we tell it that the current commit is bad:

```
> git bisect start
SESA560987@DESKTOP-D21661F ▶ C:\GitHub\BisectTest ⑂ main ↑12
> git bisect bad
```

Figure 11.5: Starting bisect

Now we need to tell it a good commit. Let's look at the log:

```
> git lg
51dbcca | Test real division [Jesse Liberty]  (7 minutes ago)  (HEAD → main, refs/bisect/bad)
6a9f37b | Using the modulus operator [Jesse Liberty]  (9 minutes ago)
a196d78 | Test 23/4 in integer division [Jesse Liberty]  (13 minutes ago)
6f4cf1d | Add square root [Jesse Liberty]  (19 minutes ago)
38fc64a | Add real division [Jesse Liberty]  (19 minutes ago)
fb07de9 | Add modulus operator [Jesse Liberty]  (22 minutes ago)
49431f9 | Add the divide function [Jesse Liberty]  (24 minutes ago)
652a690 | Add the multiply function [Jesse Liberty]  (25 minutes ago)
351b39d | Add the subtract function [Jesse Liberty]  (26 minutes ago)
7ae0b2d | Add the add function [Jesse Liberty]  (27 minutes ago)
e7e308c | Add calculator class [Jesse Liberty]  (29 minutes ago)
174a008 | Create the project [Jesse Liberty]  (34 minutes ago)
7259bb3 | Initial commit [Jesse Liberty]  (41 minutes ago)  (origin/main, origin/HEAD)
```

Figure 11.6: Looking for the good commit

We know that the second commit was good because all we did was create the project. Let's tell that to bisect:

```
> git checkout 174a008
Note: switching to '174a008'.
```

Figure 11.7: A known good commit

You may get a lot of warnings about having a detached head (ouch). You can safely ignore those warnings. For form's sake, we'll test the currently checked-out commit and of course, it is fine. So we tell bisect that the current checkout is good:

```
> git bisect good
Bisecting: 5 revisions left to test after this (roughly 3 steps)
[49431f9b5ec1754adcc4b1647753a371fc4641ec] Add the divide function
SESA560987@DESKTOP-D21661F  C:\GitHub\BisectTest  (49431f9 ... )|BISECTING
```

Figure 11.8: Telling Bisect this commit is good

It comes back with some interesting information. It tells you that if the original commit was bad, and this one is good, then it has five revisions left to test, which will take roughly three steps. It also tells you that it checked out the commit whose message is "Add the divide function." Let's inspect the (now) current program and see if it is right. (Normally, here, you'd run the program to see if you get the expected result. Even better, you might run your suite of unit tests to see if it passes.)

Looking in Visual Studio we see that the working directory looks like this:

```
namespace BisectTest
{
    public class Calculator
    {
```

```
        public int Add(int x, int y)
        {
            return x + y;
        }
        public int Subtract(int x, int y)
        {
            return x + y;
        }
        public int Multiply(int x, int y)
        {
            return x * y;
        }
        public int Divide(int x, int y)
        {
            return x / y;
        }
    }
}
```

Looks good. Note that some functions are missing, and that is because bisect checked out an earlier commit. We can tell bisect that this commit is good:

```
> git bisect good
Bisecting: 2 revisions left to test after this (roughly 2 steps)
[6f4cf1d761bced5c521fb14b5710ae603fcd6c0a] Add square root
SESA560987@DESKTOP-D21661F ▶ C:\GitHub\BisectTest ⟩ ⌖ (6f4cf1d ... )|BISECTING ≢
```

Figure 11.9: Another good commit

It comes back and says that we've really narrowed things down. There are only two revisions left to test. Look at the original log:

```
> git lg
51dbcca | Test real division [Jesse Liberty]  (7 minutes ago)  (HEAD → main, refs/bisect/bad)
6a9f37b | Using the modulus operator [Jesse Liberty]  (9 minutes ago)
a196d78 | Test 23/4 in integer division [Jesse Liberty]  (13 minutes ago)
6f4cf1d | Add square root [Jesse Liberty]  (19 minutes ago)
38fc64a | Add real division [Jesse Liberty]  (19 minutes ago)
fb07de9 | Add modulus operator [Jesse Liberty]  (22 minutes ago)
49431f9 | Add the divide function [Jesse Liberty]  (24 minutes ago)
652a690 | Add the multiply function [Jesse Liberty]  (25 minutes ago)
351b39d | Add the subtract function [Jesse Liberty]  (26 minutes ago)
7ae0b2d | Add the add function [Jesse Liberty]  (27 minutes ago)
e7e308c | Add calculator class [Jesse Liberty]  (29 minutes ago)
174a008 | Create the project [Jesse Liberty]  (34 minutes ago)
7259bb3 | Initial commit [Jesse Liberty]  (41 minutes ago)  (origin/main, origin/HEAD)
```

Figure 11.10: The repo to demonstrate bisect

We told it that the latest is bad and the second is good. We then were offered the commit whose message is "Add the divide function." That is, bisect cut our list of commits roughly in half and checked out a commit for us to test. We told bisect that the commit it had us try was good. So, Bisect thinks, "Hmm. Divide is good, and real division is bad, so let's cut it in half (giving us "Add square root") and see if that is good or bad. Either way, we only have one more test to get the final answer."

When we try the code, it is bad; it does not work in the expected way. So, let's tell Bisect that square root is bad. In response, it checks out "Add real division." Look again at the log. Either this one is bad or the one below it is bad. We've already told it that "Add the divide function" is good, and we've already told it that the square root commit is bad:

```
> git bisect bad
Bisecting: 0 revisions left to test after this (roughly 1 step)
[38fc64a7ee715eeb5a01544f36a057fa536c0137] Add real division
```

Figure 11.11: Honing in on the problem

It has checked out "Add the divide function" so let's test that.

That one is bad, so we'll tell bisect that:

```
> git bisect bad
Bisecting: 0 revisions left to test after this (roughly 0 steps)
[fb07de9f5ebf963f6eae57c020efa6a1613655d1] Add modulus operator
```

Figure 11.12: We have found the problem

It comes back and tells us that "Add modulus operator" must be the culprit and that there is nothing more to test. We've got it. Let's look – sure enough, the modulus operator is using the divide operator instead:

```
public int Modulus(int x, int y)
{
    return x / y;
}
```

Even though we had to use a simple and fake example, you can see how bisect narrows down the commits to find the first one that went bad. Now that we know what is wrong, we can fix it.

Blame

This unfortunately-named command can be a great help in tracking down who made changes to your code, line by line. From there you can talk with the programmer and discover their intention, or provide an opportunity for correction.

To open Blame in Visual Studio, right-click on a file and choose **Git** and then **Blame**. The file will open with a section on the left that will list who made the edit to that line of code.

Challenge

Create a program with twenty commits. Put an error in one of the early commits that won't break the working program (so that it can be hidden). Use bisect to find the error.

The first step is to create a program with 20 commits. I decided to create a program that holds information about a book:

```
namespace BisectTest
{
    public class Book
    {
        public string Author { get; set; }
        public string BookName { get; set; }
        public double Price { get; set; }
        public double DiscountPrice { get; set; }
        internal double WholeSalePrice { get; set; }
        internal double DiscontinuedPrice { get; set; }

        public void ComputePrice()
        {
            Price = WholeSalePrice + (WholeSalePrice * .5);
        }

        public void ComputeDiscountPrice()
        {
            DiscountPrice = Price * 2;
        }
```

```
        public void ComputeDiscontinued()
        {
            DiscontinuedPrice = DiscontinuedPrice * 0.8;
        }


    }
}
```

We also have a program that interacts with our book class and displays the results:

```
using System;

namespace BisectTest
{
    class Program
    {
        static void Main(string[] args)
        {
            var book = new Book();
            book.Author = "Jesse Liberty";
            book.BookName = "Pro Git for Programmers";
            book.WholeSalePrice = 10.0;
            book.ComputePrice();
            Console.WriteLine($"{book.BookName} by {book.Author}" );
            Console.WriteLine($"{book.BookName}: {book.Price}");
            Console.WriteLine($"Discount price is
              {book.DiscountPrice}");
            Console.WriteLine($"Discontinued price is
              {book.DiscontinuedPrice}");
        }
    }
}
```

Let's run the program and examine the output:

```
Pro Git for Programmers by Jesse Liberty
Pro Git for Programmers: 15
Discount price is 0
Discontinued price is 0
```

That is clearly not what we intended. Both the discount and the discontinued prices are 0, where they should be a fraction of 15. Oh! We forgot to call the method to compute the prices. When we do, and we display them all, we get this:

```
Pro Git for Programmers by Jesse Liberty
Pro Git for Programmers: 15
Pro Git for Programmers discount price = 30
Discontinued price is 0
```

Better, but still not right. Why is Discontinued coming out to zero? To find this, we'll use bisect. To start we'll enter:

```
git bisect start
```

Next, we need to tell Bisect that the current (most recent) commit is bad by entering:

```
git bisect bad
```

Looking at the log, I see that the first commit has the ID 7259bb3. So we'll enter:

```
Git checkout 7259bb3
Git bisect good
```

It checks out a version for me to test, and tells me that there are 11 revisions to test after this (assuming this is bad) and that it will take roughly 4 steps. We continue bisecting until we find the first instance of the broken code, as we saw above.

12

Fixing Mistakes

The most common reaction to making a mistake in Git is to panic. What if you have just lost all your work? Worse, what if you have broken the master branch?

This chapter will review a number of common Git mistakes and how to fix them. The first rule, of course, is stay calm, or as Douglas Adams said, *Don't Panic!*

The problems we'll review are:

- You wrote the wrong message in a commit.
- You forgot to add changed files from your last commit.
- Problems with the order of commits or their messages.
- You need to undo changes made in a commit.
- You misnamed your branch.
- You committed to the wrong branch.
- You trashed a file in a previous commit.
- You messed up the remote by pushing a broken branch.

To see the answers at work, let's mirror Panofy into ErrorsDemo. Here are the steps we'll be doing:

1. On the remote, create ErrorsDemo and get its URL.
2. Go to the local branch you want to mirror (in our case, Panofy).
3. Push that up to the server with the mirror command, using ErrorsDemo's URL.
4. Clone the new branch (be sure to clone it in the directory you want it).
5. Change directory to the new (cloned) directory (ErrorsDemo).

You can see this walked through in *Chapter 10, Important Git Commands & Metadata.*

You wrote the wrong message in the last commit

Let's start with the log so that we can see the change:

```
jesse@Win10   ~  source  repos  errorsdemo  main ≡
> git lg
* 4b080ba - (HEAD → main, tag: ReleaseCandidate, origin/main, origin/HEAD) change name of
  csproj to correct name (4 weeks ago) <Jesse Liberty>
* 8d47c04 - add converter skeleton (10 weeks ago) <Jesse Liberty>
* 2ca4ad9 - add subtract method (10 weeks ago) <Jesse Liberty>
* 877348c - Update csproj (10 weeks ago) <Jesse Liberty>
* c507abf - Add Hello message (10 weeks ago) <Jesse Liberty>
* 3c9929c - Sync'ing with B (10 weeks ago) <Jesse Liberty>
* 2661adc - fix conflicts (10 weeks ago) <Jesse Liberty>
|\
| * da77c91 - First use of Panofy in Dir B (10 weeks ago) <Jesse Liberty>
* | edd7b01 - Initial files from DirA (10 weeks ago) <Jesse Liberty>
|/
* a253788 - Initial commit (10 weeks ago) <Jesse Liberty>
```

Figure 12.1: Log of initial state

This one is easy; all you need do is enter:

```
git commit --amend
```

Your editor will open and allow you to change the message. To change the wording of the message just change the "pick" to "reword."

After you save your file, the message of the last commit will be changed as shown in *Figure 12.2*:

```
> git lg
* 0b9f686 - (HEAD → main) change name of csproj (2 minutes ago) <Jesse Liberty>
* 8d47c04 - add converter skeleton (10 weeks ago) <Jesse Liberty>
* 2ca4ad9 - add subtract method (10 weeks ago) <Jesse Liberty>
* 877348c - Update csproj (10 weeks ago) <Jesse Liberty>
```

Figure 12.2: Log after amend (changed message in the last commit)

You forgot to add changed files from your last commit

You solve this problem in the exact same way you solved the problem of fixing the message in your last commit: with --amend.

First, stage your new or changed files. Then enter:

```
git --amend
```

If you don't want to edit the message when you add the files, enter:

```
git --amend --no-edit
```

Problems with the order of commits or their messages

If the problem is not with the last commit (in which case you'd use --amend), it's time to break out interactive rebase as shown in *Chapter 8, Interactive Rebasing*. If you haven't pushed yet, Interactive Rebase will let you do all this and more.

You need to undo changes made in a commit

All you need to do here is to call the log, get the ObjectID of the commit you want to undo and call:

```
git revert ObjectID
```

Let's go back to the log:

```
> git lg
* 0b9f686 - (HEAD → main) change name of csproj (2 minutes ago) <Jesse Liberty>
* 8d47c04 - add converter skeleton (10 weeks ago) <Jesse Liberty>
* 2ca4ad9 - add subtract method (10 weeks ago) <Jesse Liberty>
* 877348c - Update csproj (10 weeks ago) <Jesse Liberty>
* c507abf - Add Hello message (10 weeks ago) <Jesse Liberty>
* 3c9929c - Sync'ing with B (10 weeks ago) <Jesse Liberty>
* 2661adc - fix conflicts (10 weeks ago) <Jesse Liberty>
|\
| * da77c91 - First use of Panofy in Dir B (10 weeks ago) <Jesse Liberty>
* | edd7b01 - Initial files from DirA (10 weeks ago) <Jesse Liberty>
|/
* a253788 - Initial commit (10 weeks ago) <Jesse Liberty>
```

Figure 12.3: Log, starting point

Now let's revert the commit that added the hello message:

```
git revert c507abf
```

Because I reverted a change in the middle of the branch, it's no surprise that I run into a merge conflict:

```
> git revert c507abf
Auto-merging Panofy/Panofy/Program.cs
CONFLICT (content): Merge conflict in Panofy/Panofy/Program.cs
error: could not revert c507abf ... Add Hello message
hint: after resolving the conflicts, mark the corrected paths
hint: with 'git add <paths>' or 'git rm <paths>'
hint: and commit the result with 'git commit'
```

Figure 12.4: Merge conflict

To solve this I will call git mergetool, invoking the tool I set up in *Chapter 4, Merging, Pull Requests, and Handling Merge Conflicts*. Kdiff3 is smart enough to fix all the conflicts without my help:

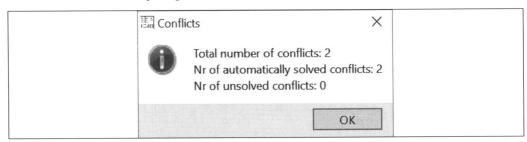

Figure 12.5: Kdiff3 fixes the conflicts for me

Sure enough, when we open Program.cs the Hello World is gone:

```
namespace Panofy
{
    19 references | Jesse Liberty, 66 days ago | 1 author, 4 changes
    public class Program
    {
        0 references | Jesse Liberty, 66 days ago | 1 author, 4 changes
        static void Main(string[] args)
        {
            Console.WriteLine("Another output line");
        }
    }
}
```

Figure 12.6: Program.cs after revert

You misnamed your branch

Checkout the branch in question and enter:

```
git branch -m <currentName> <desiredName>
```

Here's what we get:

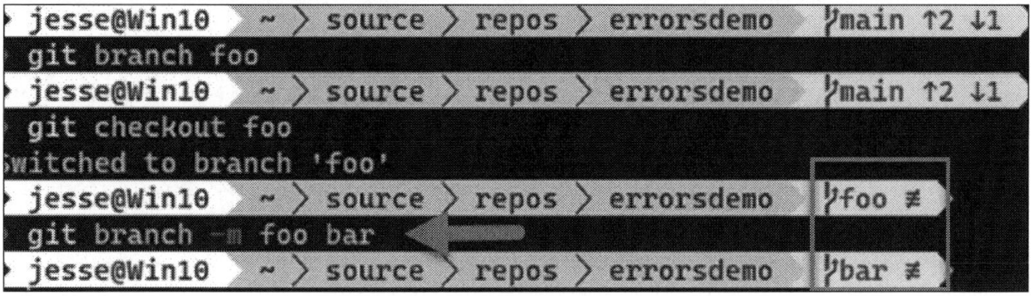

Figure 12.7: Renaming branch foo to bar

In *Figure 12.7* you create the branch foo and then check it out. Finally, you rename it as shown above and your branch name is changed.

You committed to the wrong branch

The way this plays out for me (again and again!) is that I forget to create a new branch and so make my changes on the develop branch or to main. To fix this, enter:

```
git branch <new branch>
git reset HEAD~ --hard
```

You are creating the new branch, then removing the check-in from main (HEAD~) but leaving the files in the new branch.

You trashed a file in a previous commit

You ruin a file but you only find out about it after a number of other commits. Ouch. Use git log to find the ObjectID for a commit from *before* the problem commit. Now we want to get only that file from the commit. For this, we enter:

```
git checkout ObjectID -- <path to file>
```

(The path to the file is relative to the root of the project.)

You now have the earlier version in the staging area. You can "unstage" it and edit it from the work area.

An alternative to using the ObjectID is to count back from HEAD, such as:

```
git checkout HEAD~4 --<path to file>
```

This just says "go back 4 commits and get the file from there." The two approaches work equally well.

You messed up the remote by pushing a broken branch

If (and when) you break the Master branch by pushing an incomplete and broken local copy, dry your tears, take heart! This can be fixed.

Note, this should not be possible. If you are using Azure DevOps (or something similar) your pipeline should not accept any merge that doesn't compile (and arguably pass a set of unit tests). But I digress…

The first command you want is:

```
git reset --hard <remoteRepository> / <Yourbranch>@{1}
```

That resets your local copy of <Yourbranch> to the last synchronized version of <remoteRepo>. Thus, if your branch is Feature1 and it is on origin, you would write:

```
git reset --hard origin/Feature1@{1}
```

Now you want to restore the remote repo to its state before you broke it:

```
git push -f <remoteRepository><Yourbranch>
```

Quiz

The challenge for this chapter consists of a quiz. The answers are all at the end of the quiz.

1. What do you do if you left out a changed file in the last commit?
2. What do you do if you committed to the wrong branch?
3. What do you do if you corrupted a file in a previous commit?
4. What do you do if you need to undo changes made in a commit?
5. What do you do if you trash Master by pushing a broken branch?

Answers

What do you do if you left out a changed file in the last commit?

You solve this with the same command you use to modify the message in the last commit, using --amend, but you need to indicate that you do not want to edit the message (make sure your files are staged):

```
git --amend --no-edit
```

What do you do if you committed to the wrong branch?

Checkout or create the branch you want to have committed to and then use reset to remove the change from the remote branch, but leave your files in the index (staging area) to be committed to the new branch:

```
git branch <new branch>
git reset HEAD~ --hard
```

What do you do if you corrupted a file in a previous commit?

First, use git log to find a commit before the corruption. Get the ObjectID of that commit. Next, get the problem file (and only that file) from the good commit:

```
git checkout ObjectID -- <path to file>
```

Remember: The path to the file is relative to the root of the project.

You now have the healthy version of the file in the staging area. If that file needs editing you can unstage it, but the more likely case is that you can use this older version as is. In that case, you can just commit it.

What do you do if you need to undo changes made in a commit?

In this case, open the log and get the ObjectID of the commit you want to undo. You can now call revert on that ObjectID:

```
git revert ObjectID
```

What do you do if you trashed Master by pushing a broken branch?

If your DevOps system allowed you to push a broken branch to Master, fix this immediately. In fact, if you can, tell the rest of your team not to commit to Master until you fix it. After they stop yelling at you, do this:

```
git reset --hard <remoteRepository> / <Yourbranch>@{1}
```

That resets your local copy of <Yourbranch> to the last synchronized version of <remoteRepo>. Thus, if your branch is myFeature and it is on origin, you would write:

```
git reset --hard origin/myFeature@{1}
```

Now you need to restore the remote repo to its state before you broke it:

```
git push -f <remoteRepository><Yourbranch>
```

Master should now be fixed.

Great job with the quiz! Keep this chapter around for the inevitable day you will need it.

13
Next Steps

Over the course of this glorious book, you have learned about:

- Installing Git at the command line, within Visual Studio, and GitHub Desktop
- How to create a remote repository on GitHub
- How to clone a repository to your local repository using the command line, Visual Studio, or GitHub Desktop
- How to pull changes down to the local repository
- How to push changes up to the remote repository (origin)
- Best practices on the frequency of committing
- How to write effective messages when committing
- What the work area is
- What the stash is
- What the index/staging area is
- What the local repository is
- What the remote repository is
- How to stage and commit
- How to commit without staging
- What branches are and how to create them
- How to push a new branch
- What the HEAD pointer is

- How to examine your commits with Log
- How to push a commit to the server
- How to manage your commits with the command line, Visual Studio, and GitHub Desktop
- How to merge into the main branch
- What a pull request is
- What merge conflicts are and how to resolve them
- What a Fast Forward merge is
- What a True Merge is
- What Rebasing is and how to use it
- How to use amend to modify the previous commit
- How to cherry-pick commits from one branch to another
- How to work with Interactive Rebasing to change history
- The standard workflow using Git
- What notes are and how to use them
- What tags are and how to use them
- Using the `log` to review your commits
- Using log flags and commands to zero in on the information you want
- How to see the information the log provides in Visual Studio and GitHub Desktop
- Using Diff to see what has changed
- Using aliases to save time and simplify your use of Git
- Searching for words or phrases in a set of commits
- Creating the stash
- Listing what's in the stash
- Retrieving from the stash
- The `clean` command for getting rid of unwanted untracked files
- How to see metadata and choose which data you want to see
- Using bisect to find a broken commit
- Using blame to examine which programmer made each change to a file
- Fixing numerous kinds of errors

Despite this seemingly comprehensive list, there are some advanced or corner cases that we did not cover. Further, there are additional flags for almost all the commands we did cover. You can learn about them in several places. The key locations for learning about Git are:

- GitHub Docs Repository: `https://github.com/github/docs`
- Git users mailing list: `http://jliberty.me/gitmail`
- Stack Overflow: `http://jliberty.me/SOGit`
- Git Documentation reference: `http://jliberty.me/GitDocs`

You can reach me at `jesseliberty@gmail.com` if none of these resources answer your question, though I'm sometimes slow to respond.

The Git commands should not change much, if at all, and Visual Studio and GitHub Desktop will almost certainly keep up with any changes as they arrive.

Be sure to check out some of the other excellent GUI interfaces to Git, such as:

- Fork
- SourceTree
- Tortoise Git

There are too many to list, but take a look at `http://jliberty.me/GitGUI` for a nearly exhaustive list of GUI clients.

Good luck and I hope you Git everything you want in life.

Jesse Liberty

`http://jesseliberty.com`

`@jesseliberty`

Other Books You May Enjoy

If you enjoyed this book, you may be interested in these other books by Packt:

Expert Python Programming – Fourth Edition

Michał Jaworski

Tarek Ziadé

ISBN: 978-1-80107-110-9

- Explore modern ways of setting up repeatable and consistent Python development environments
- Effectively package Python code for community and production use
- Learn about modern syntax elements of Python programming, such as f-strings, dataclasses, enums, and lambda functions
- Demystify metaprogramming in Python with metaclasses
- Write concurrent code in Python
- Monitor and optimize the performance of Python application
- Extend and integrate Python with code written in different languages

Learning Tableau 2020 - Fourth Edition

Joshua N. Milligan

ISBN: 978-1-80020-036-4

- Develop stunning visualizations to explain complex data with clarity

- Explore exciting new Data Model capabilities

- Connect to various data sources to bring all your data together

- Leverage Tableau Prep Builder's amazing capabilities for data cleaning and structuring

- Create and use calculations to solve problems and enrich the analytics

- Master advanced topics such as sets, LOD calculations, and much more

- Enable smart decisions with data clustering, distribution, and forecasting

- Share your data stories to build a culture of trust and action

Packt is searching for authors like you

If you're interested in becoming an author for Packt, please visit authors.packtpub. com and apply today. We have worked with thousands of developers and tech professionals, just like you, to help them share their insight with the global tech community. You can make a general application, apply for a specific hot topic that we are recruiting an author for, or submit your own idea.

Share your thoughts

Now you've finished *Git for Programmers*, we'd love to hear your thoughts! Scan the QR code below to go straight to the Amazon review page for this book and share your feedback or leave a review on the site that you purchased it from.

https://packt.link/r/1-801-07573-5

Your review is important to us and the tech community and will help us make sure we're delivering excellent quality content.

Index

Made in the USA
Middletown, DE
25 July 2021